AF255177

Bees of California: Art, Science, and Poetry

ISBN 978-0-692-08966-8

Copyright © 2018 Hamutahl Cohen

Edited by Hamutahl Cohen & Juniper Harrower
Book Design by Sofia Vermeulen
Book Cover by Sofia Vermeulen

Published by SymbioStudio with assistance from the UCSC Norris Center for Natural History.

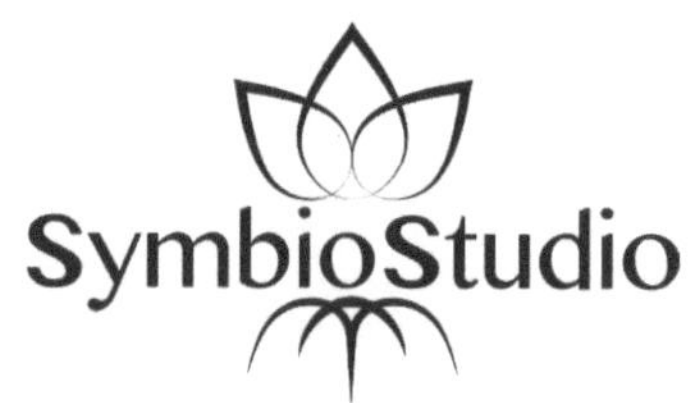

BEES
OF CALIFORNIA
ART SCIENCE POETRY

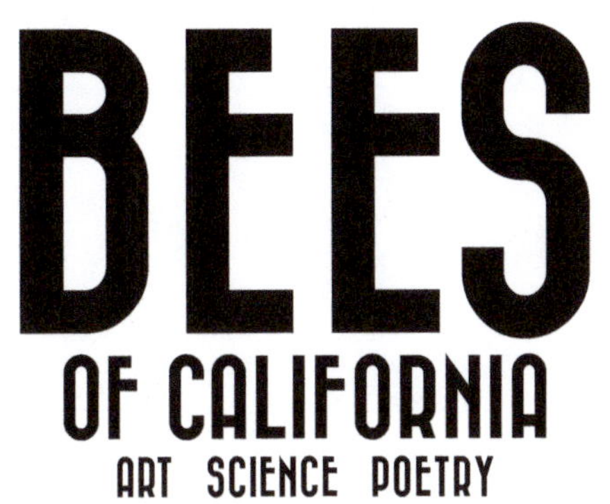

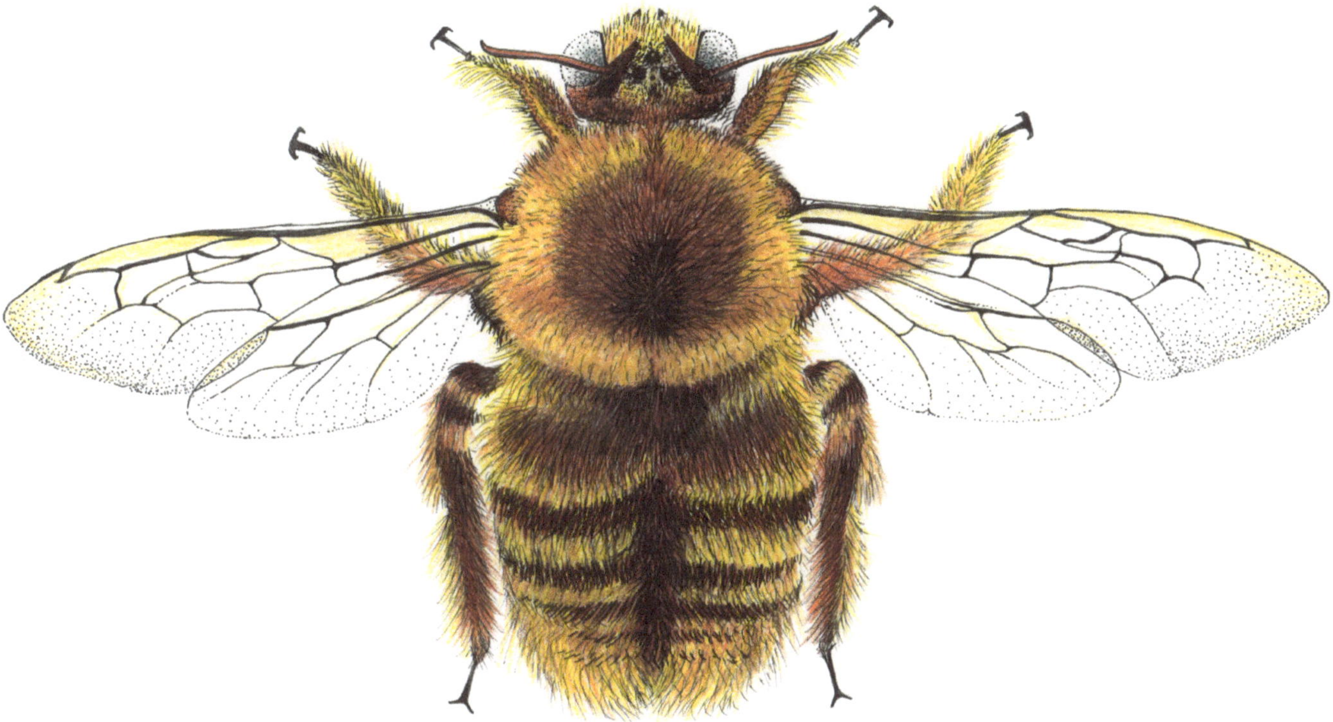

EDITED BY HAMUTAHL COHEN & JUNIPER HARROWER
DESIGNED BY SOFIA VERMEULEN

WITH CONTRIBUTIONS BY 30 STUDENTS FROM UNIVERSITY OF CALIFORNIA, SANTA CRUZ

This book was inspired by the illustrations of Summer-Solstice Thomas. In 2015, Summer joined our research team at UC Santa Cruz as a high school intern. With her infectious love of bees, she showed us that drawing insects was a form of both study and tribute. Many others at the university came together to help make this book a reality - from poetry and art instructors who lent us their class time (Mattias Lanas and Courtney Kersten) to the staff and faculty of the Norris Natural History Center at UCSC (Chris Lay and Karen Holl). This project would not be possible without generous support from the UCSC IDEA Hub, a campus wide program to support social and creative student-led initiatives. Thank you to the extremely talented Sofia Vermuelen, a promising young artist who designed this book. She is sure to make a buzz in whichever artistic endeavors she pursues. Finally, we want to acknowledge all the student illustrators and poets who contributed their art to this collection.

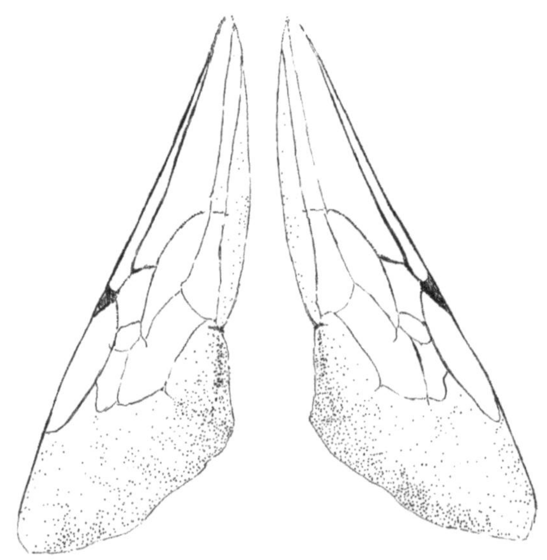

CONTENTS

CONTRIBUTORS

The contributors to this book are students and their instructors at the
University of California, Santa Cruz.

STUDENT ARTISTS:
Grace Ackles (29)
Caroline Brandt (37)
Aliya Cacanindin (57)
Hannah Caisse (13, 52, 53, 60)
Yusen (Alan) Coa (8)
Haley Coopergard (25)
Charlotte Grenier (3, 31)
Camille Hartley (58)
Nina Ibarra (34)
Jessie James (64)
Andi Juarez (23)
Rachel Lazansky-Weast (27)
Janelle Manlapas (55)
Mariam Moazed (35)
Willow Moseley (43)
Elexis Padrón (66)
Michelle Pastor (41)
Vanessa Phaphone (51)
Olivia Ronan (3, 7)
Jen Samis (45)
Sofia Vermeulen (9, 10, 11, 19, 21, 62)

STUDENT POETS:
Natalie Anderson (18, 48)
Nadya Ahmadi (40)
Cody Avery (42)
Ryan Donnelly (30)
Carly Harrower (54)
Thaïs Miller (36)
Allyson Paul (26)
Alex Perrotti (52)
Annie Stert (44)
Kelsey Taylor (16, 20, 22, 24, 28, 34, 50)

INSTRUCTORS:
Mattias Lanas (49)
Juniper Harrower (17, 56)
Hamutahl Cohen (text)

INTRODUCTION

A big, fuzzy bee visits a flower in search of food. The flower is bright and colorful: the bee sees patterns on each petal (invisible to the human eye) that have evolved over thousands of years, she cannot help but be enticed. Although the bee is specially equipped to collect pollen, it is a messy business: pollen sticks to the hairs between her eyes, between her wings, and under her abdomen. As the bee moves between flowers, so does the pollen. The flower is fertilized. This action is called pollination and it is essential for human survival, allowing for the amazing diversity of fruits and vegetables we eat today. The most famous pollinator is the honey bee, but there are actually over 20,000 species of bees in the world and California is home to over sixteen hundred of them.

Cataloguing our pollinators is important because bee populations worldwide are declining. Taken alone, neither art, poetry, nor science do justice to this insect upon which our life depends. But together, they offer an homage to California's bees - their shapes, colors, behaviors, and favorite flowers. This book provides a snapshot of some of the commonly found families and species in our backyard. The text, illustrations, and haikus in this book were contributed by students and their instructors at the University of California, Santa Cruz. Spanning multiple disciplines, ages, and backgrounds, we are the voice of a generation passionate about bees. We hope you'll join us.

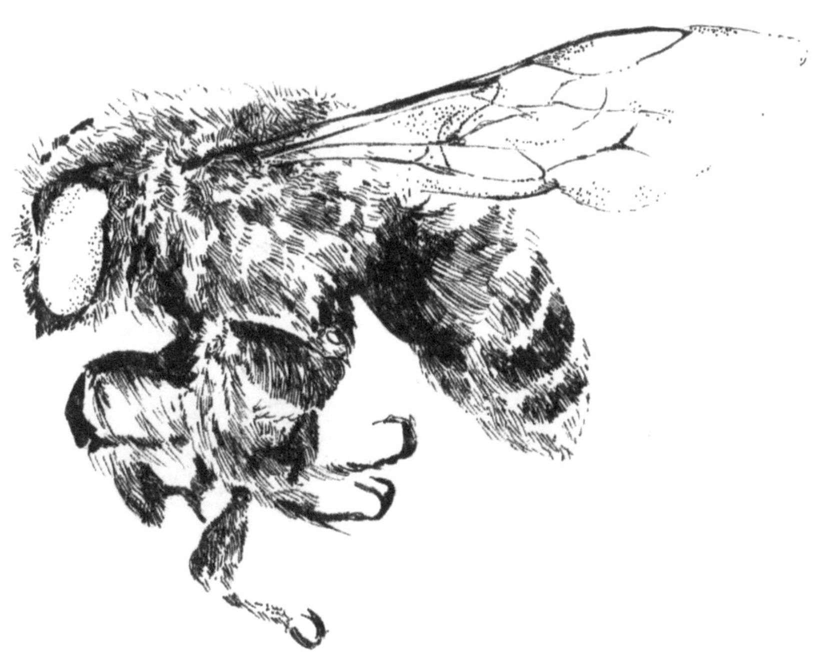

MORPHOLOGY

All bees feature specialized, branching hairs all over their body. These plumose hairs are difficult to see without a microscope, but are what differentiate bees from wasps and also make them such excellent pollinators - as bees forage for food, pollen sticks to their entire body and is transferred between flowers, ensuring pollination. With thousands of species in the world, bees also exhibit immense morphological diversity. Some bees have short, blunt tongues, while others will unfold long tongues into deep flowers. Some bees carry pollen on a pollen basket on their leg (*corbicula*), others use a dense hairbrush (*scopa*), while some do not carry pollen on their leg at all. Bees come in many shapes, colors, and sizes, from small, sleek, metallic blue bees, to large, rotund, black bees, to everything in-between.

Note that these diagrams highlight some, but not all, important features.

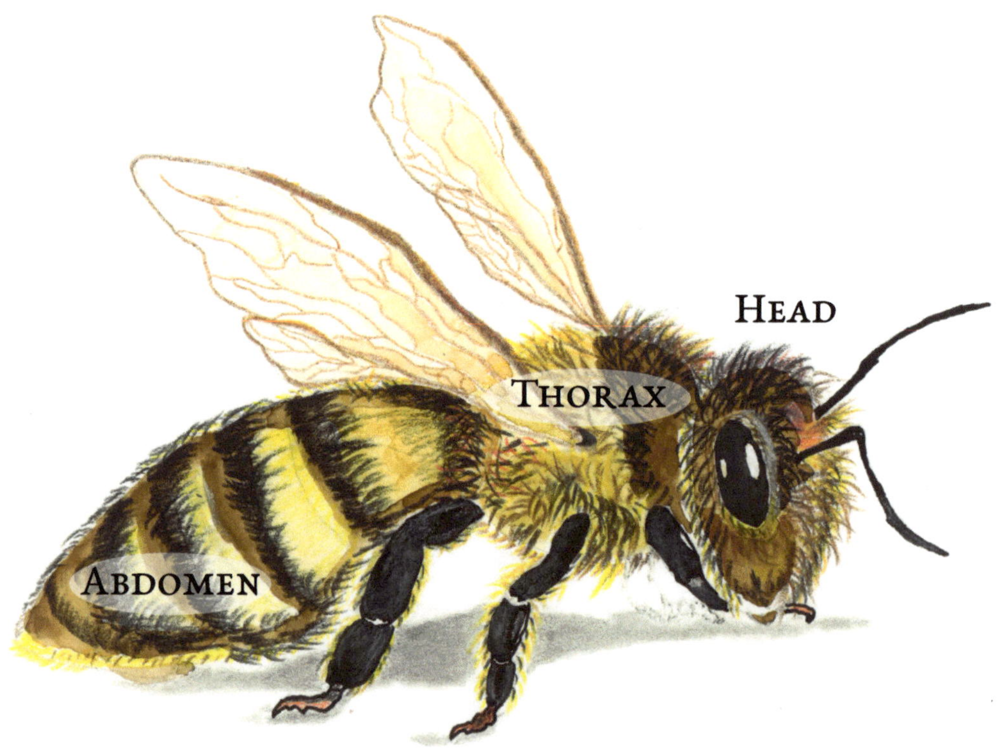

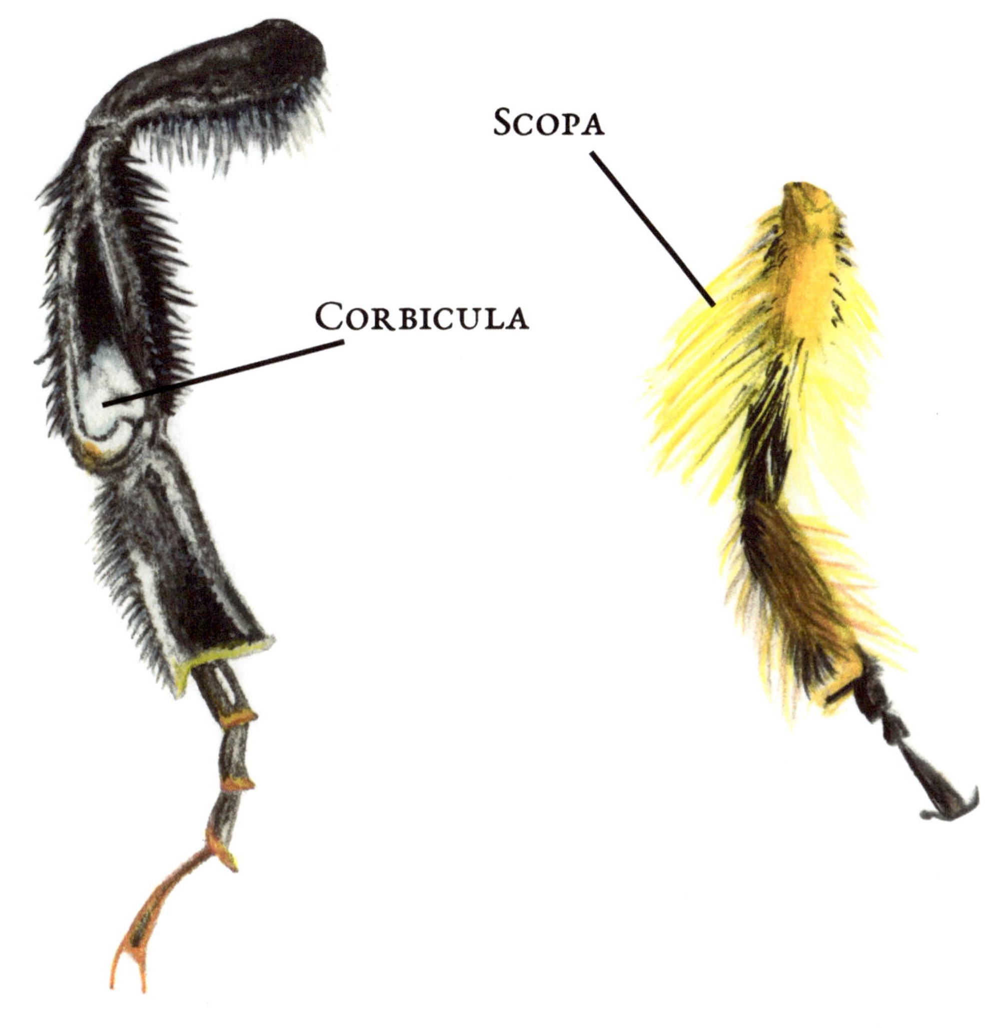

SCOPA
CORBICULA

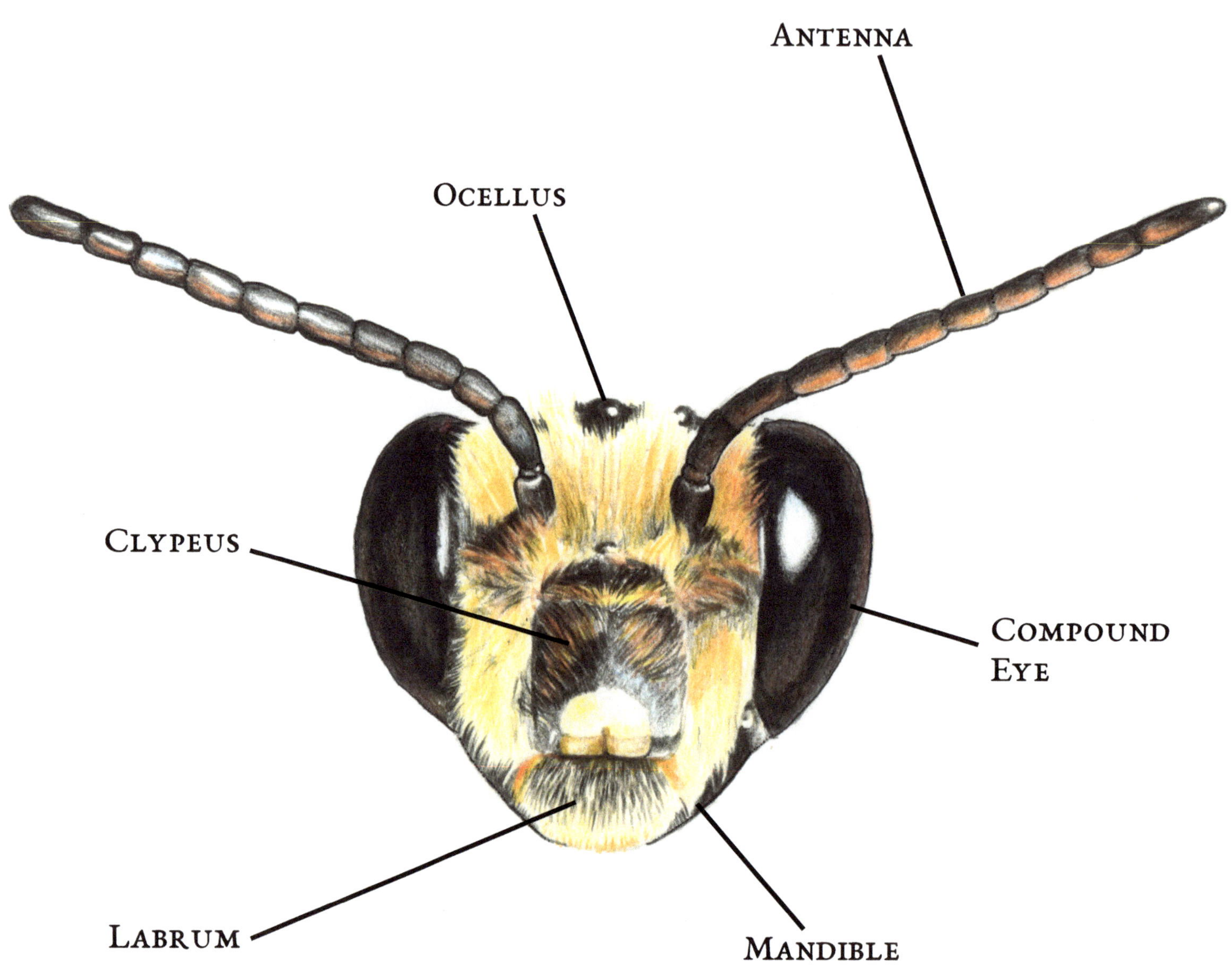

Antenna
Ocellus
Clypeus
Compound Eye
Labrum
Mandible

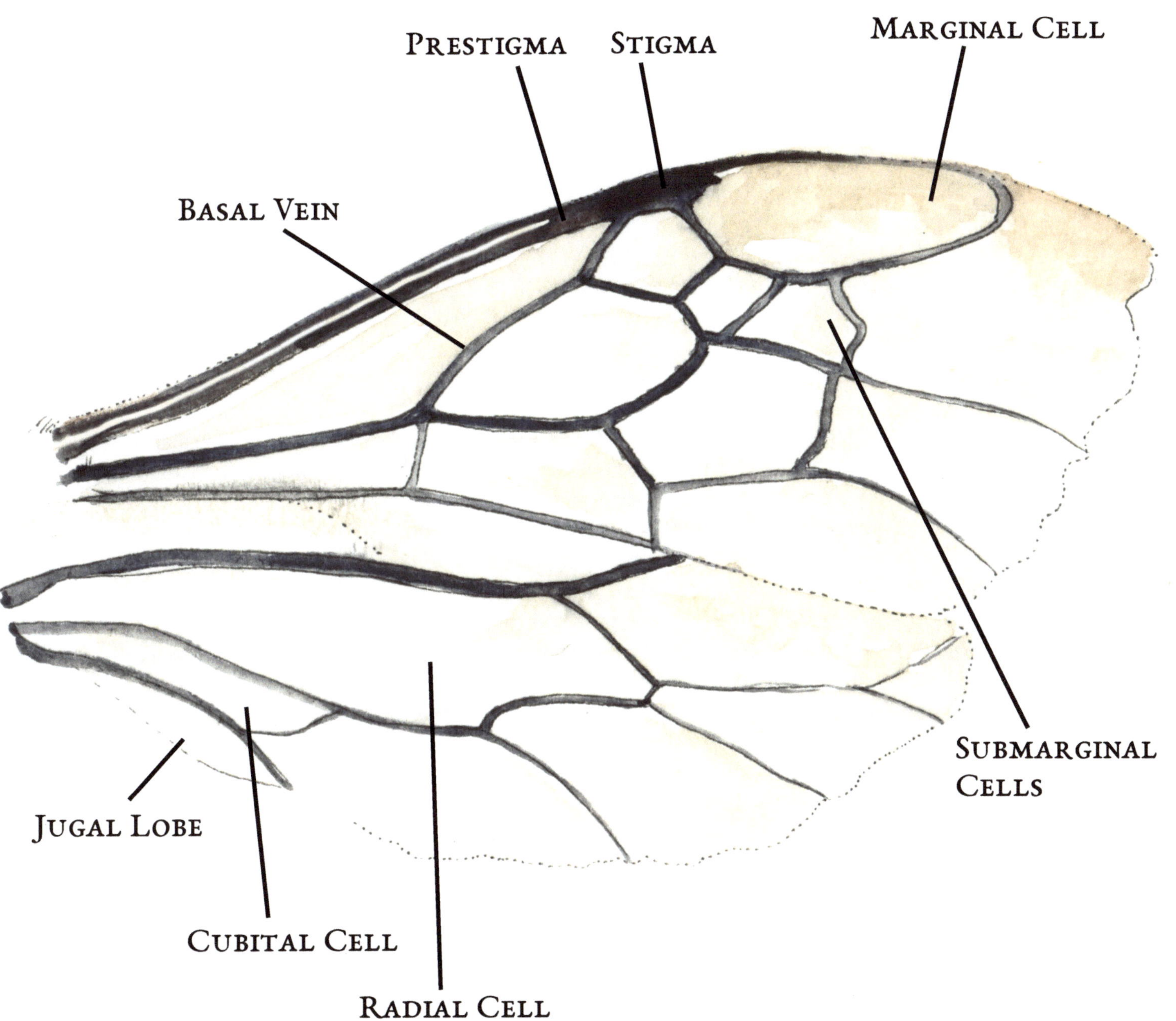

PRESTIGMA
STIGMA
MARGINAL CELL
BASAL VEIN
SUBMARGINAL CELLS
JUGAL LOBE
CUBITAL CELL
RADIAL CELL

SOCIAL BEHAVIORS

We see the full gamut of social behaviors in bees, from totally solitary bees to those that have evolved to live in large communities. Approximately 75% of all bee species are solitary, 10% are social, and 15% are cleptoparasites.

A solitary bee lives alone in a nest that she constructs below-ground in soil or above-ground in hollow reeds, twigs, or holes in wood. Every female is fertile, so there is no division of labor between queens and worker bees for these species. Female bees provide an important pollination service as they gather pollen for their offspring, but often die before their eggs mature.

Social bees share a nest with one or more individuals, known as a colony. They exhibit a range of social behaviors such as reproductive division of labor, shared brood care, and sharing a nest with overlapping generations. Of the social bees, honey bees and bumblebees are considered truly social, or "eusocial." They live in large colonies where only the queen reproduces while the workers support the colony through division of labor.

Cleptoparasitic bees (also known as cuckoo bees!) are slender and sparsely haired, resembling wasps. A cuckoo bee will enter the nest of its host, lay an egg inside of one of the cells, and then (in most cases) leave. The parasite larva will then feed on the food that was intended for the host's offspring. These parasites can be identified by their striking color patterns and often lack a pollen carrying structure.

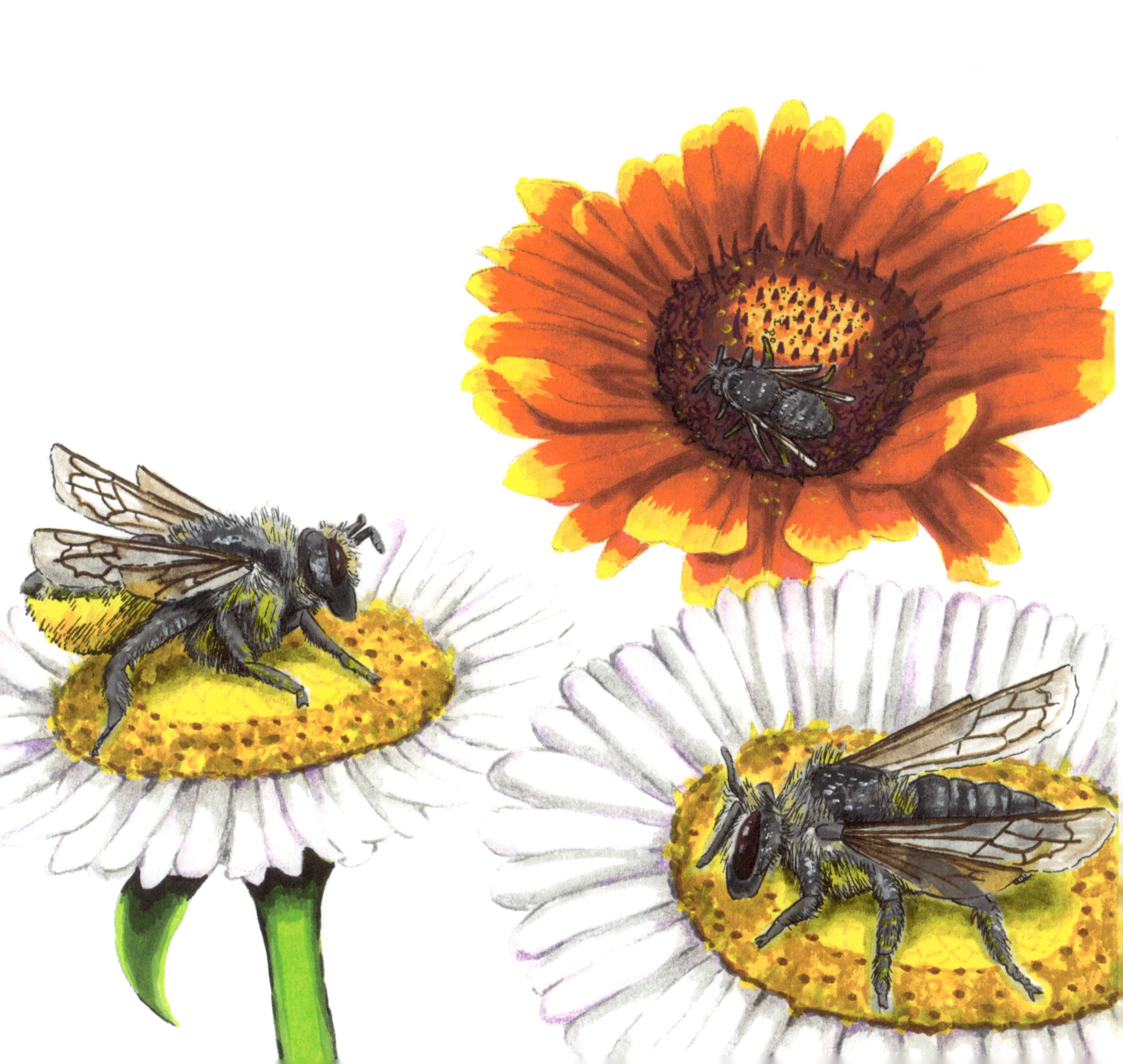

API
DAE

The Apidae family of bees includes over 5,700 species, but the most famous of all is the honey bee, *Apis mellifera*. The honey bee is golden in color, mid-sized, with a striped abdomen. The legs of the honey bee feature a basket-like scoop called a corbicula that is used to stash pollen during foraging visits. The honey bee looks similar to both the long-horned bee, *Melissodes*, as well as to the squash bee, *Peponapis*. On the flower, honey bees tend to pause and "sit," whereas both the squash bee and the long-horned bee will hover and fly, rarely pausing. The honey bee is also distinct for its highly specialized social behaviors and honey production, but it is not the only bee in the Apidae family managed for honey! -- In parts of tropical and subtropical regions, beekeepers tend to small black stingless bees which collect and store honey in small resin pots. Other important pollinators in this group include bumble bees (*Bombus*) and carpenter bees (*Xylocopa*). Both bees are big, robust, and fuzzy. Whereas bumble bees don striking black and yellow bands, female carpenter bees opt for all black, while males of some carpenter species exhibit a striking blonde. With a loud, distinct buzz, carpenter bees can often be heard before they are seen. Other genera featured in this family include the (very) small carpenter bee *Ceratina*, cream-colored *Eucera*, the sunflower bees *Diadasia*, as well as the cleptoparasite *Nomada*.

A P I S
mellifera

Get out on the flo'
& shake your ass like a bee do!
Dance this mess around.

KELSEY TAYLOR

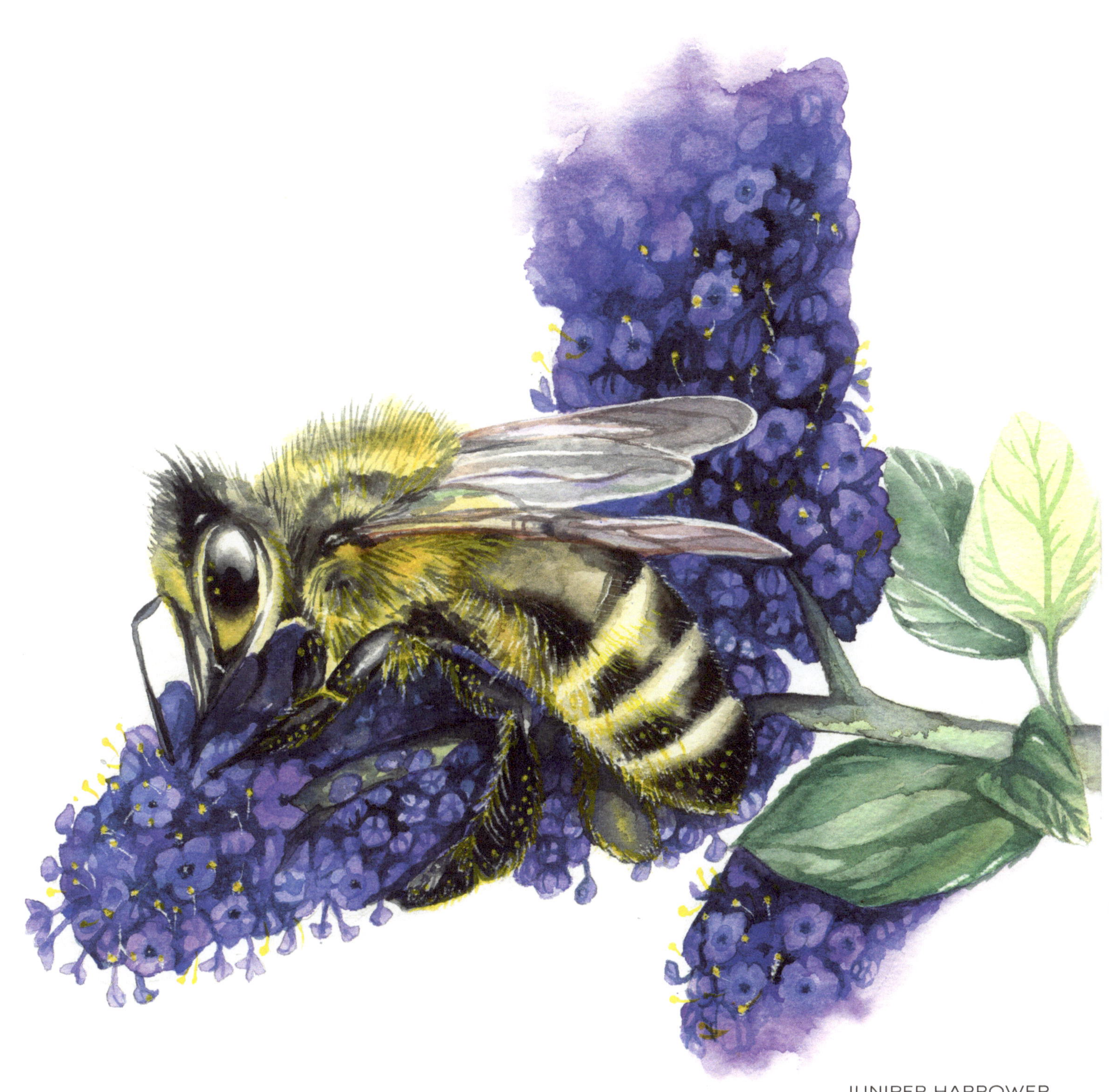
JUNIPER HARROWER

PEPONAPIS
pruinosa

Squash bees specialize
Complete floral synchronies
Connectivity

NATALIE ANDERSON

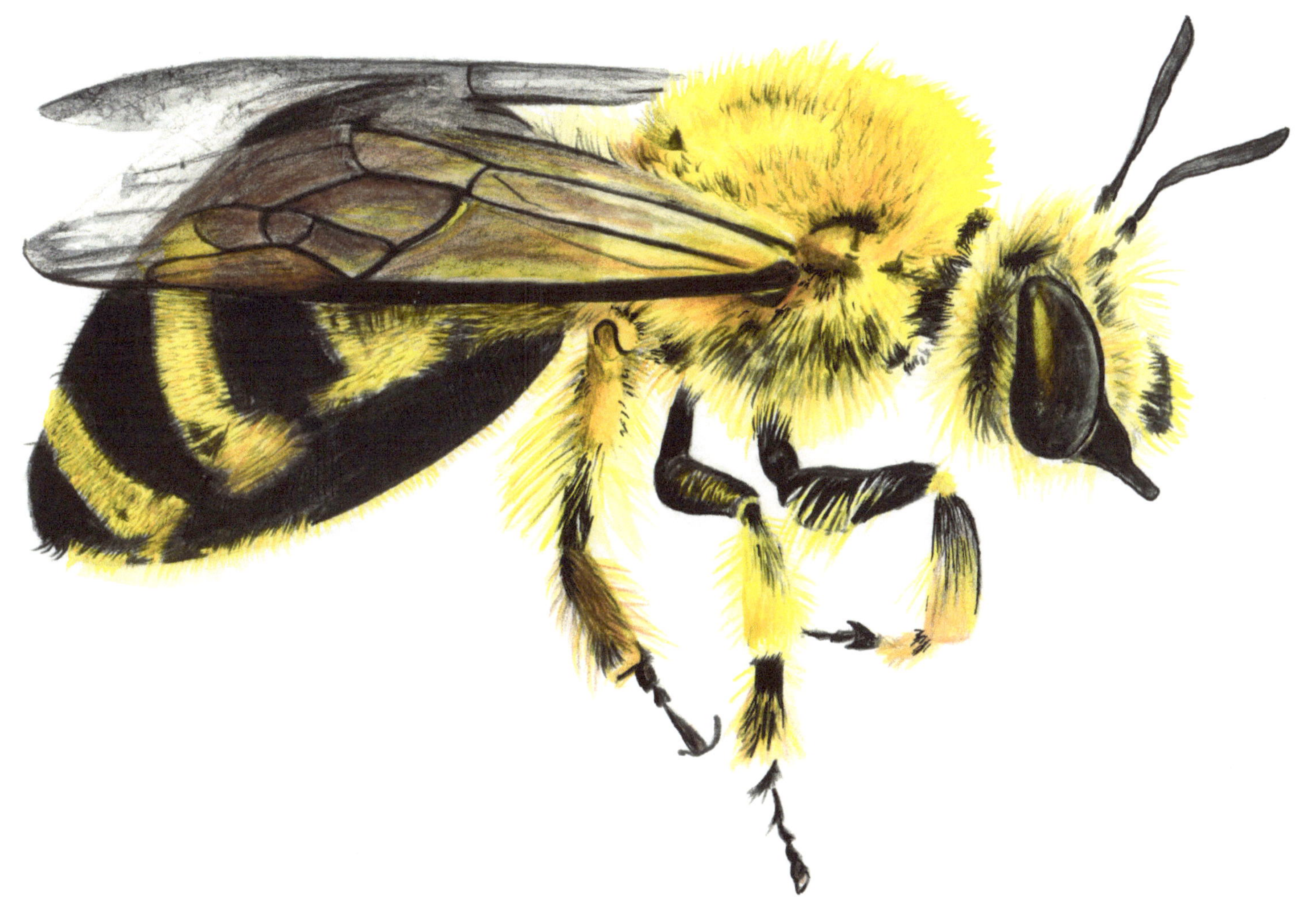

SOFIA VERMEULEN

BOMBUS
vosnesenskii

Eager for feeling
they rob nectar with loud tongue --
It breaks my study.

KELSEY TAYLOR

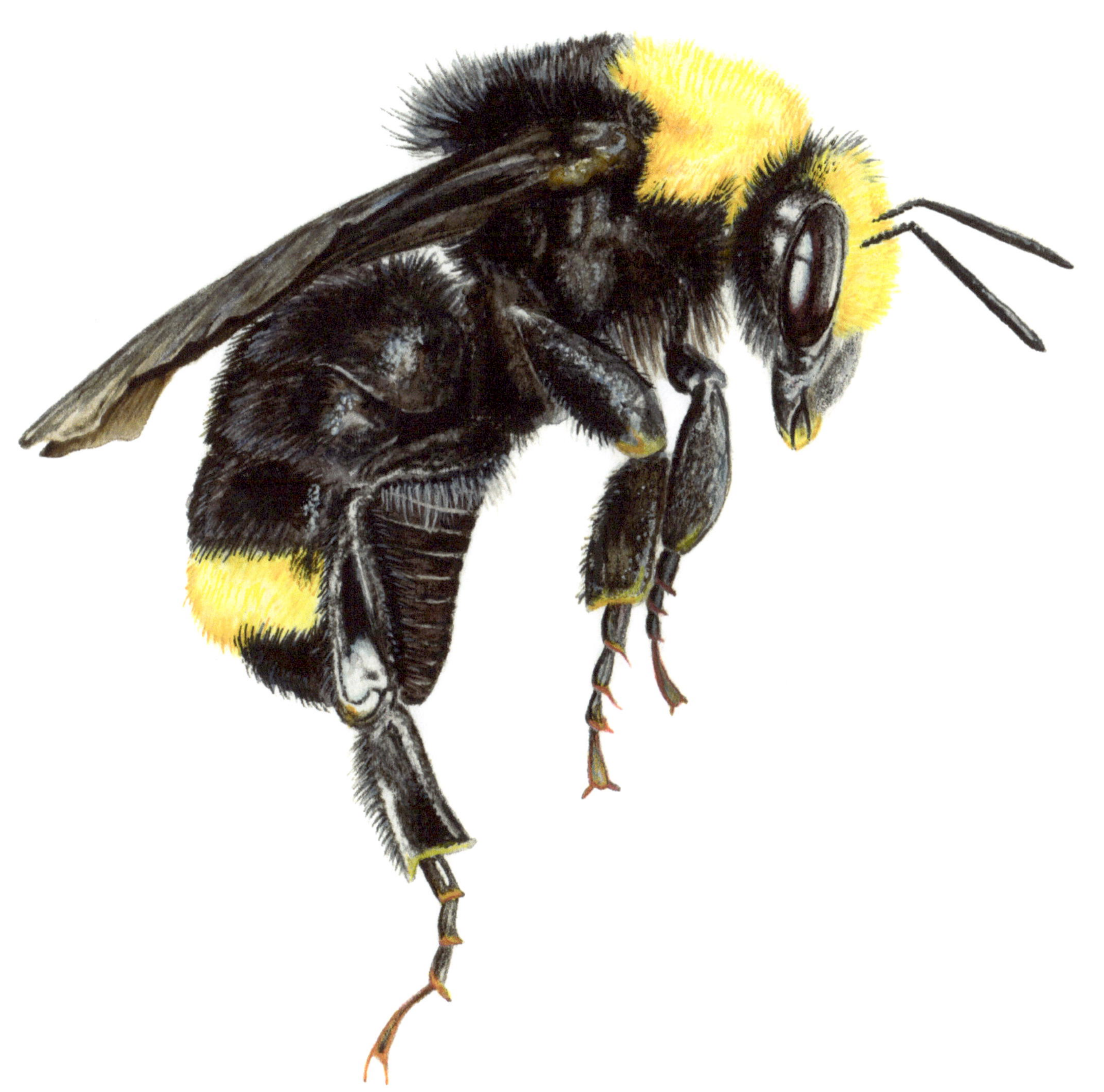

SOFIA VERMEULEN

XYLOCOPA
varipuncta

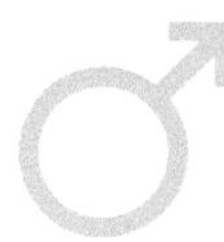

A Carpenter Bee
startles an empty daydream,
grisly but docile.

KELSEY TAYLOR

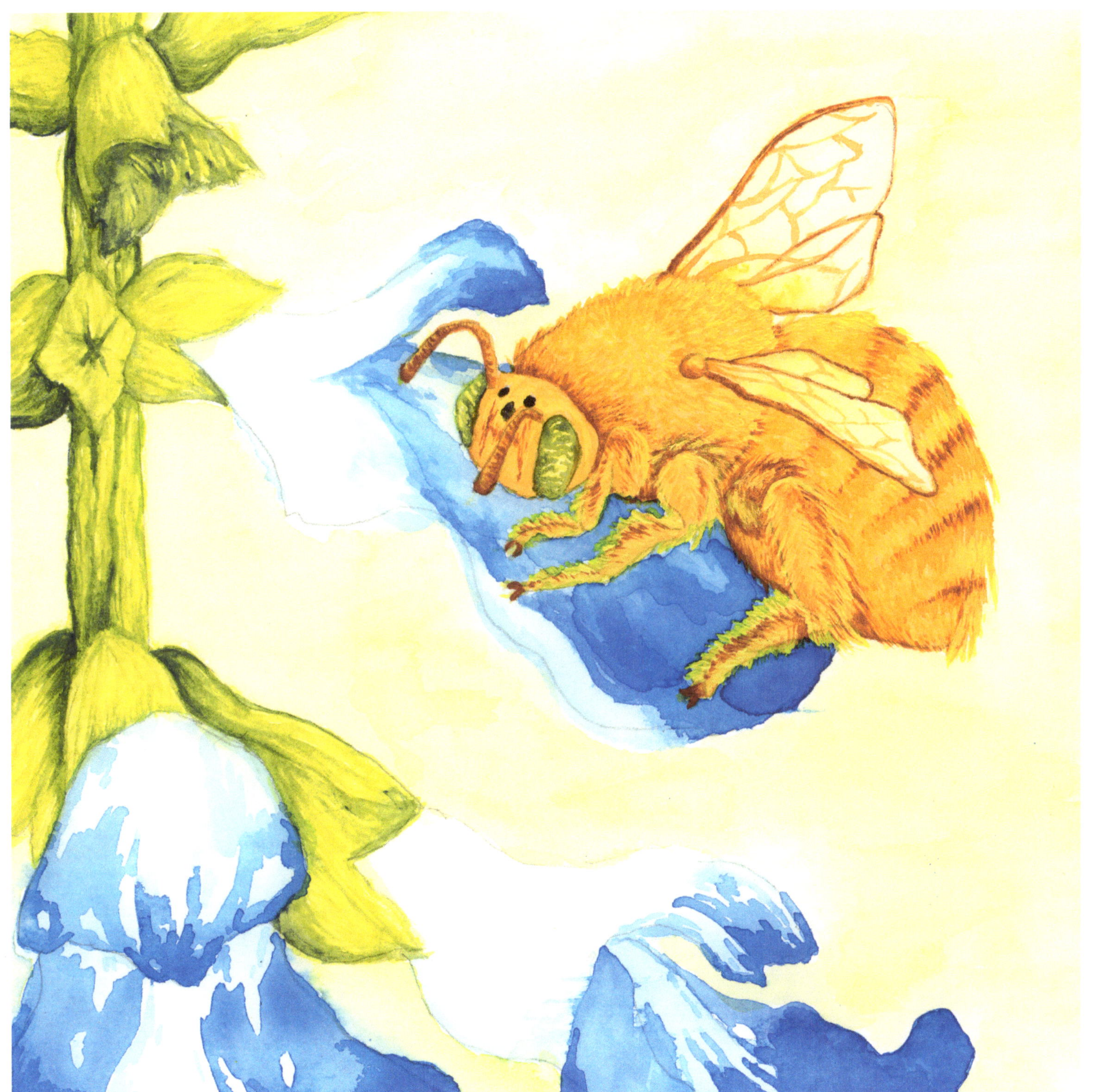

ANDI JUAREZ

XYLOCOPA
varipuncta

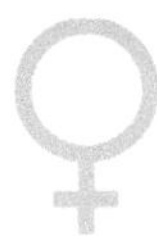

Like wing venations,
I wear my heart on my sleeves.
Translucent offbeat.

KELSEY TAYLOR

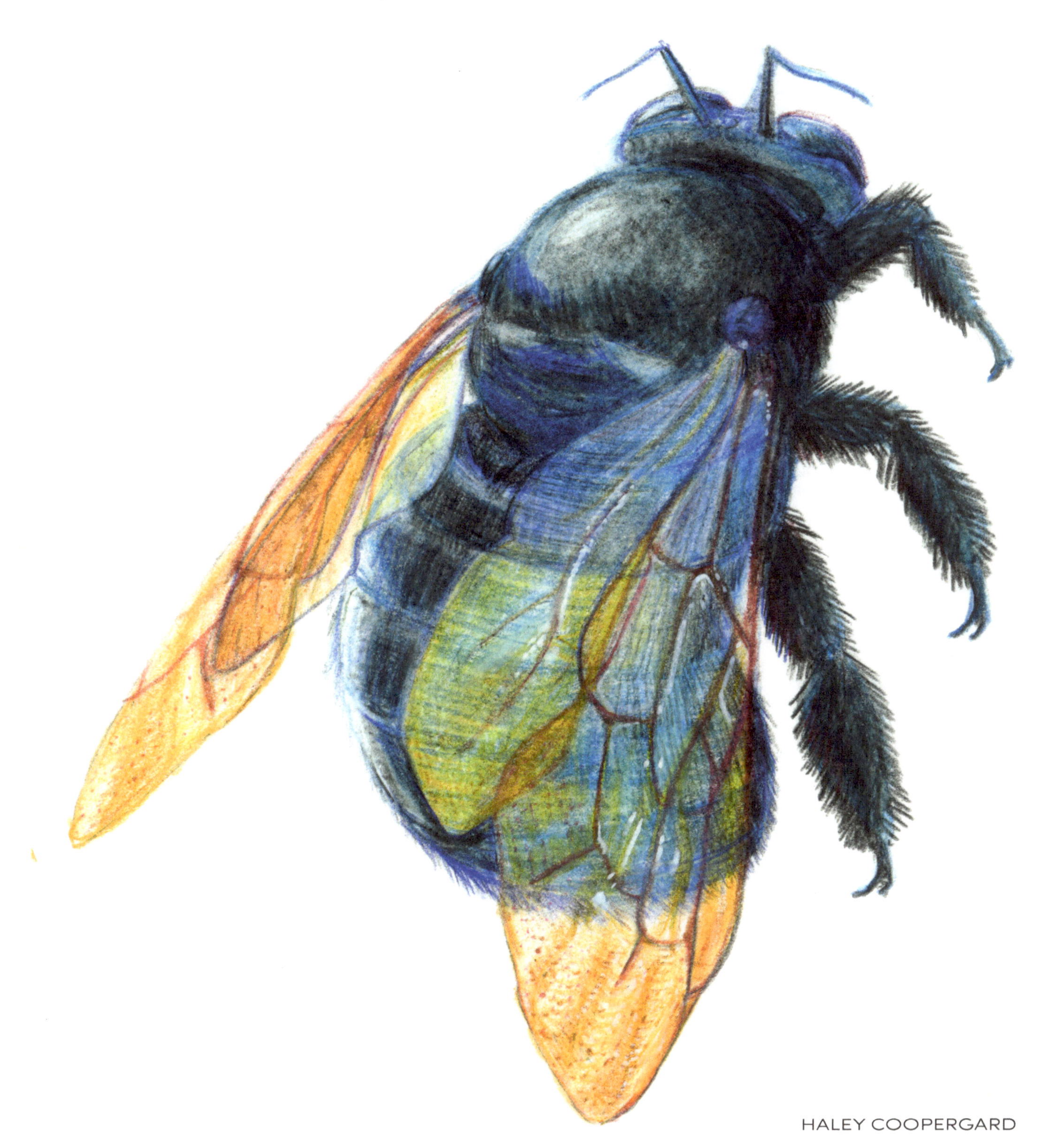
HALEY COOPERGARD

EUCERA
actuosa

The nectar became sour,
Once the bees flew south.
The flowers sang a sad song.

ALLYSON PAUL

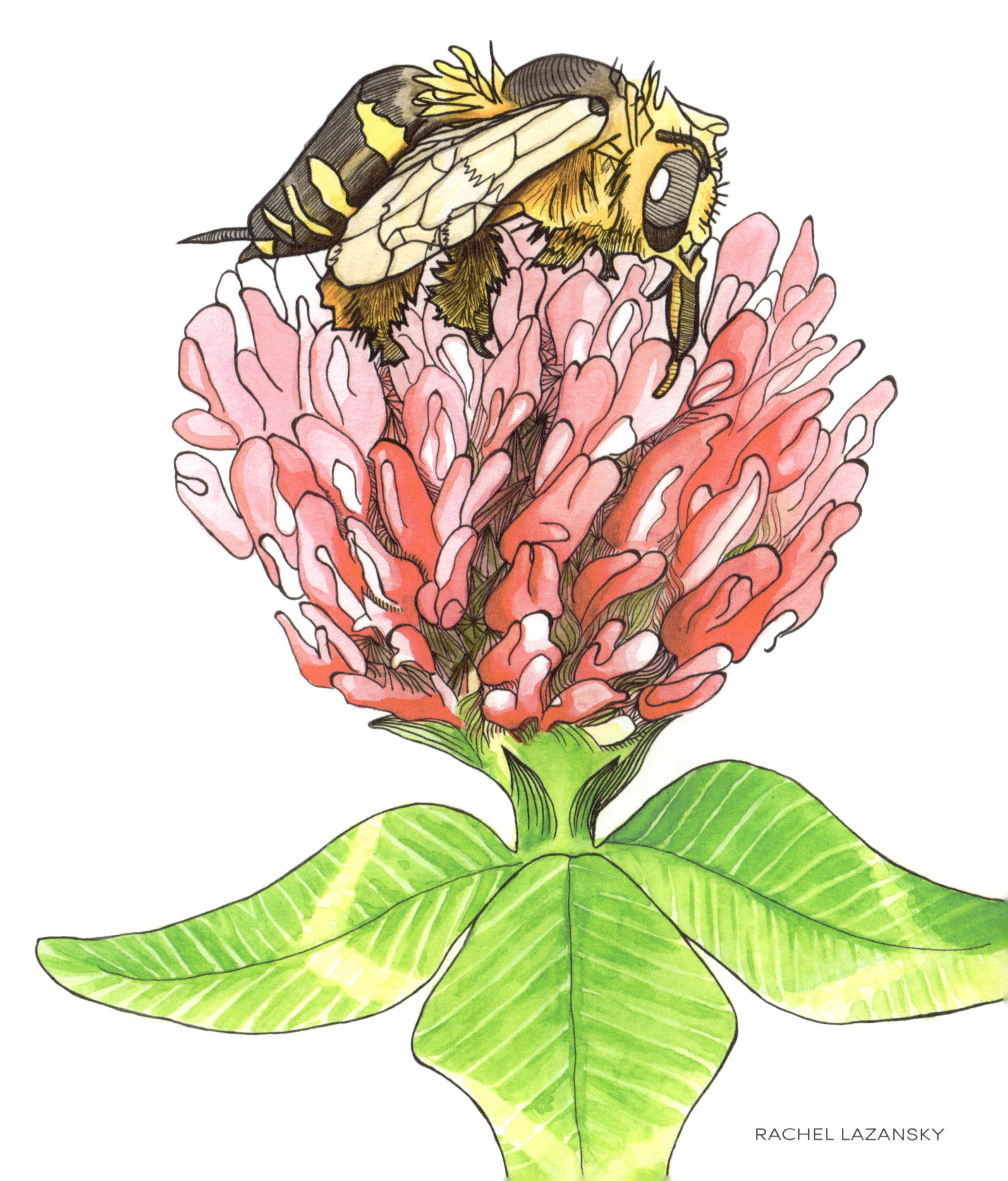
RACHEL LAZANSKY

NOMADA
edwardsii

I cling to my whits,
It clings to stock of lupine.
Together we slip.

KELSEY TAYLOR

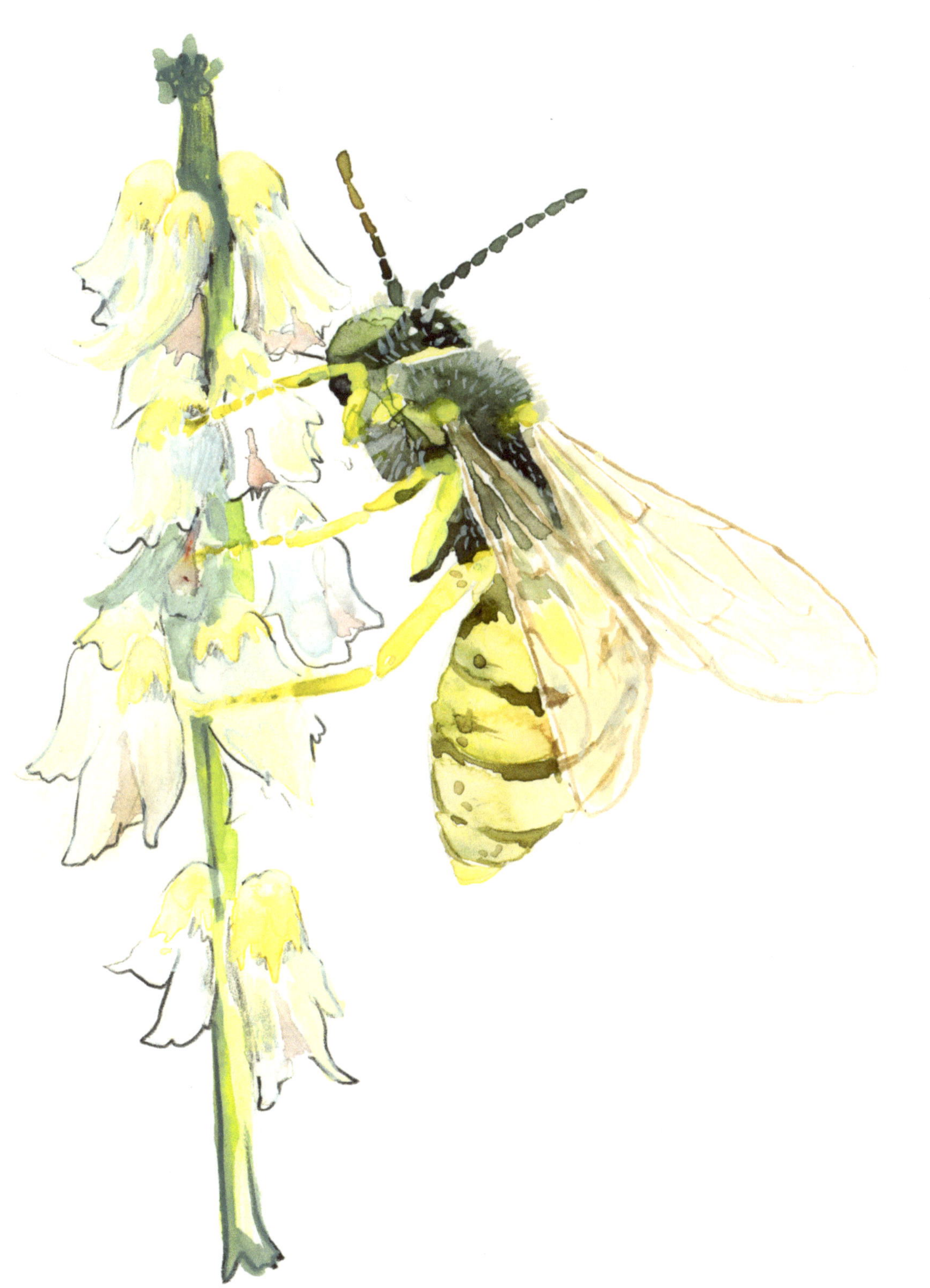

GRACE ACKLES

MELISSODES
robustior

A bee takes flight in
an unknowably big world
Lost without a queen

RYAN DONNELLY

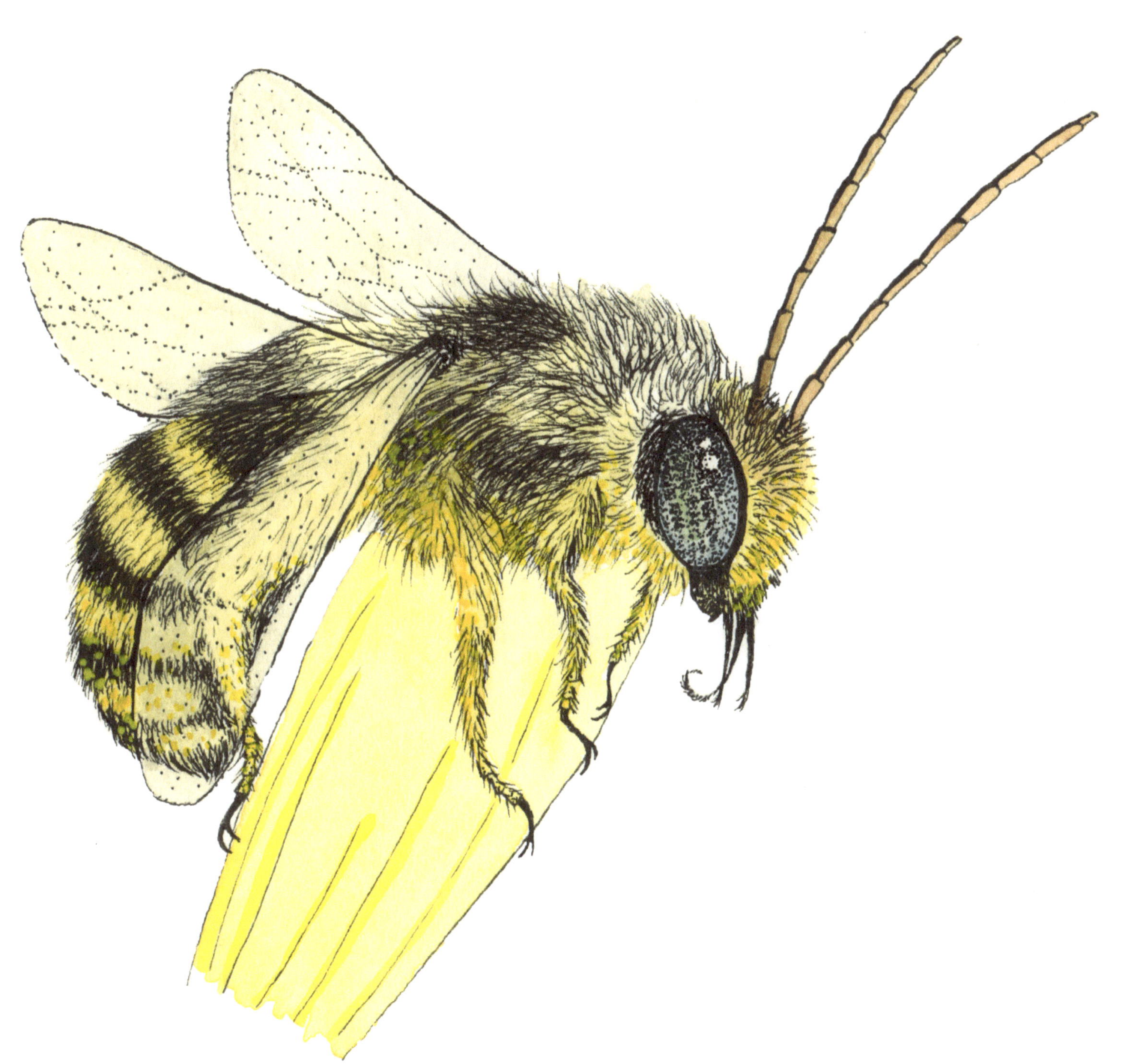

CHARLOTTE GRENIER

COLLE
TIDAE

Most bees in the Colletidae family are tiny to medium-sized and slender in build. Females will line their nests with a membranous, cellophane-like material: this is how Colletid bees earn the common name "plasterer bees." Female bees in this family have a short, blunt, bi-lobed tongue, but their small body size allows them to access deep flowers. The small, almost hairless *Hylaeus* and larger fuzzy *Colletes* are the two genera most commonly found in California. *Hylaeus* is known as the masked bee, they feature diamond shaped yellow or white markings around their eyes. They nest in pre-existing cavities in dead twigs or stems. Rather than carry their pollen on their legs, they store food in their stomach and regurgitate it upon returning to their nests for their young. *Colletes* bees excavate and construct subterranean burrows into soil. They are solitary bees, but nests are often found in aggregations together. One species of fly, the sarcophagid *Miltogramma punctatum*, is a specialist parasite of some *Colletes* species. It will follow the bee back to the nest, then deposit it's own egg in a *Colletes* cell. The fly egg hatches and eats the pollen and nectar collected by the bee for her babies, leaving them to starve.

HYLAEUS
mesillae

Mating behaviors,
social and solitary
Haste in our ventures.

KELSEY TAYLOR

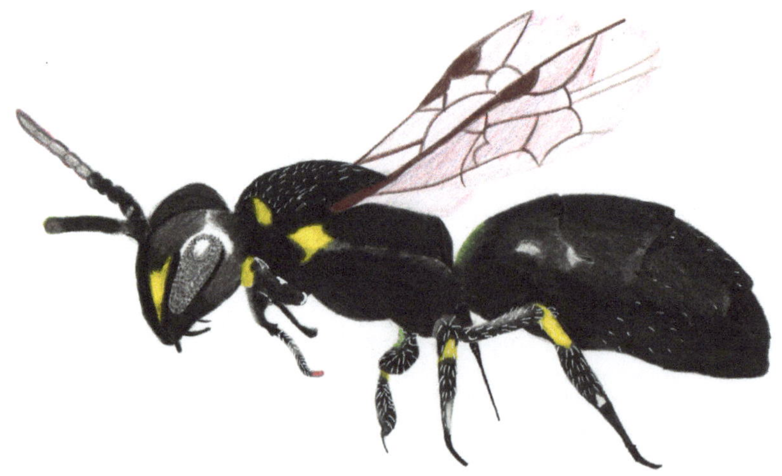

NINA IBARRA

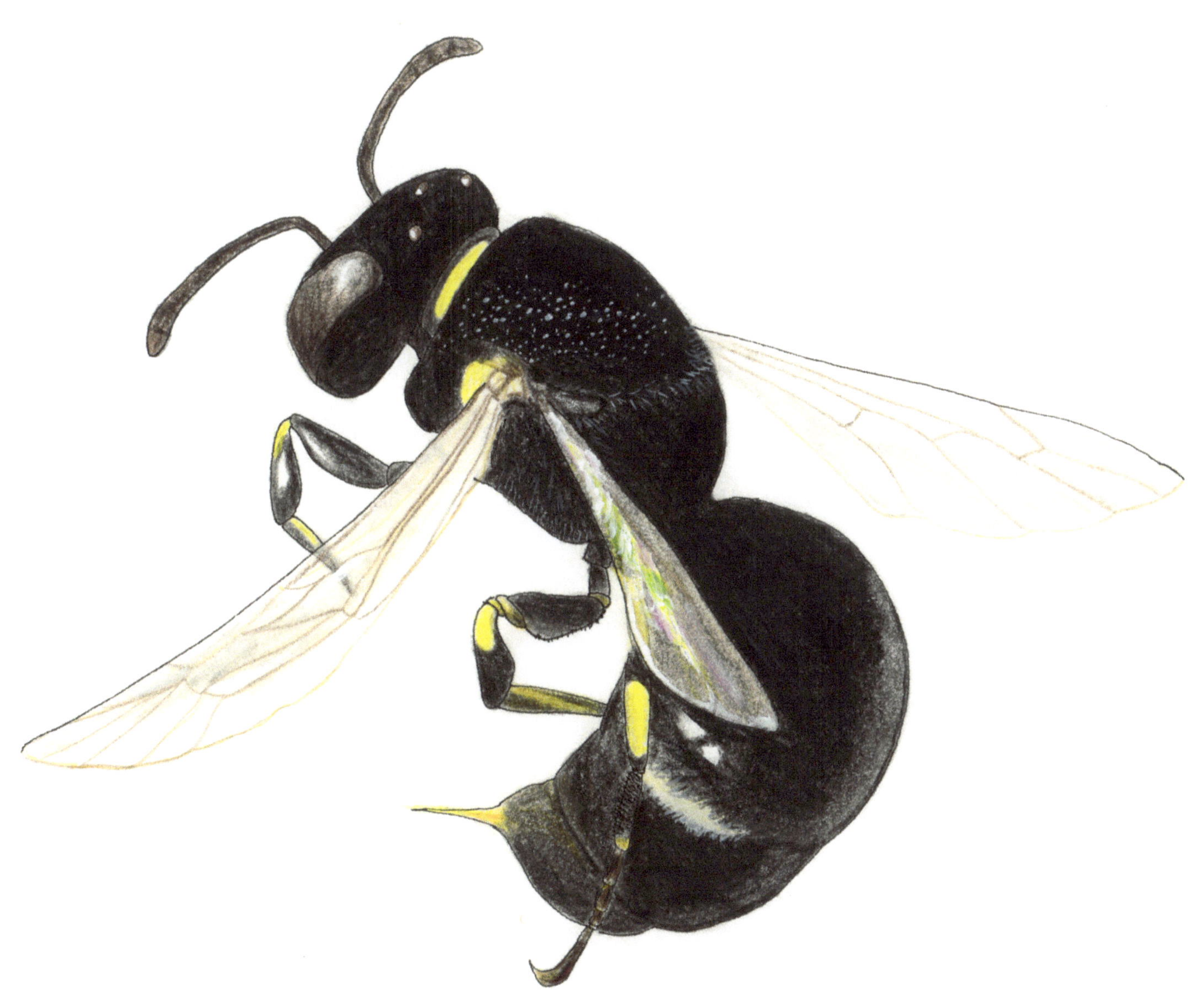

MARIAM MOAZED

HYLAEUS
punctatus

Thin film flaps the air,
Translucent silky wings flutter,
Fragile lips, kissing.

THAÏS MILLER

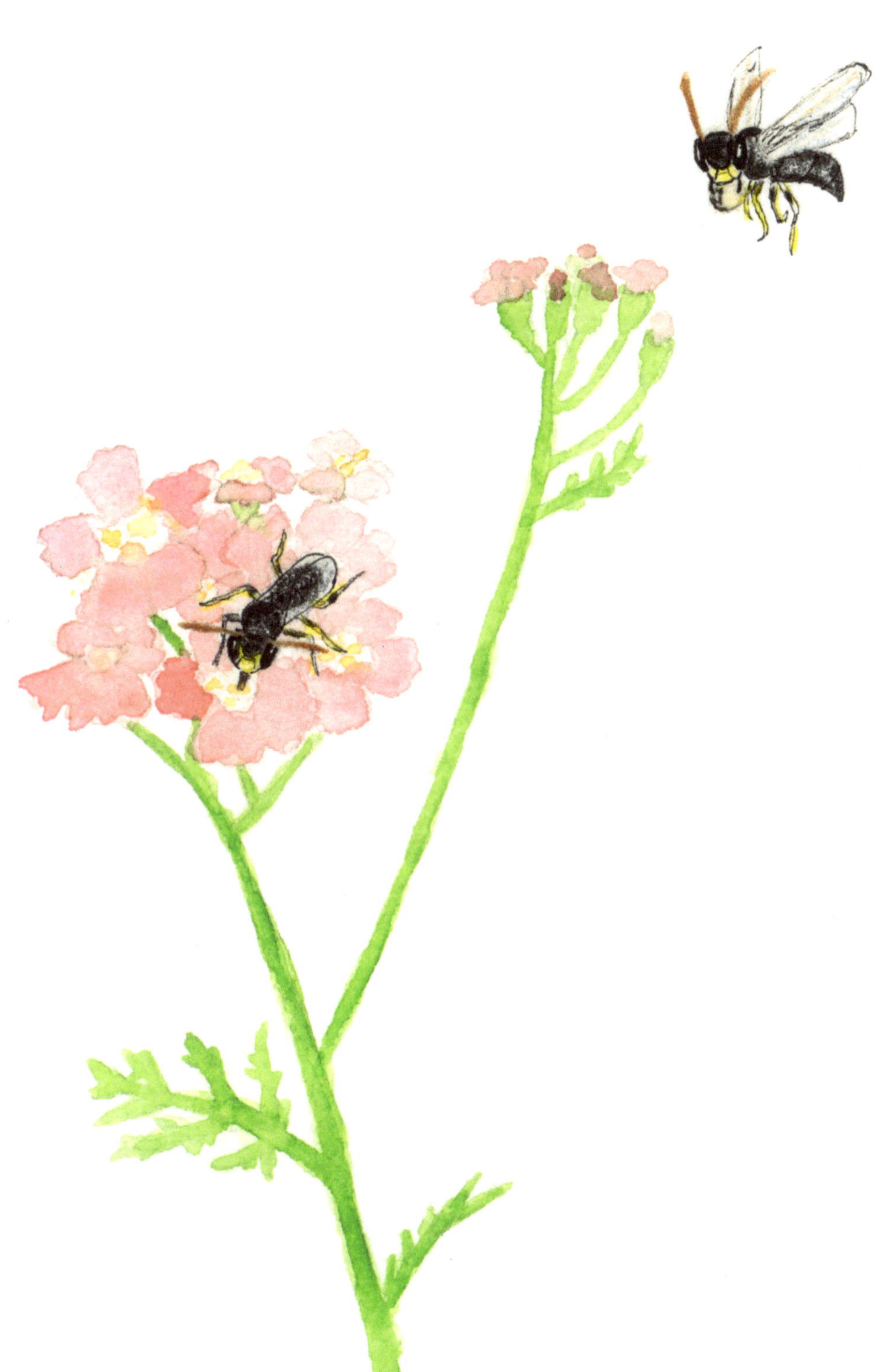

HALIC
TIDAE

Bees in the Halictidae family have an affinity for the water, salt, and minerals in human perspiration! They are thus known as the sweat bees. Next time you swat at the fly hovering near your face, make sure it's not actually a sweat bee coming in for a drink. The sweat bees are the second largest family of bees and are differentiated from other bees by unique wing venation, facial morphology, and short tongues. They are generally 5-14mm in size and slender. The *Agapostemon* bees are quite fabulous, featuring a metallic, in-your-face race car green color. Females are all green while males will show off contrasting yellow and black bands on their abdomen. This group also includes bees in the genera *Halictus* and *Lasioglossum*. These small bees are nearly identical, but can be distinguished by how hair falls on the abdomen. Bees in the Halictidae family usually nest in soil, but also sometimes in rotting wood. At their nest sites, they engage in various social behaviors. For example, several female *Agapostemon* may share a nest entrance and burrows, but each female makes and provisions her own cells with pollen and nectar for her young. And while some *Lasioglossium* species are solitary in some regions, in others, 2-3 females may share brood care tasks. This family also features several cleptoparasitic species. The female *Sphecodes* is a parasite of her fellow sweat bees. She will enter the nest of a host mother, destroy her egg, and lay her own egg in its stead to benefit from the pollen and nectar provisions already in place. Overall, halictid bees are beautiful and interesting little bees found in abundance in both California and around the world.

AGAPOSTEMON
texanus

Leave safety of hive
To pollinate and survive
And give us more life

NADYA AHMADI

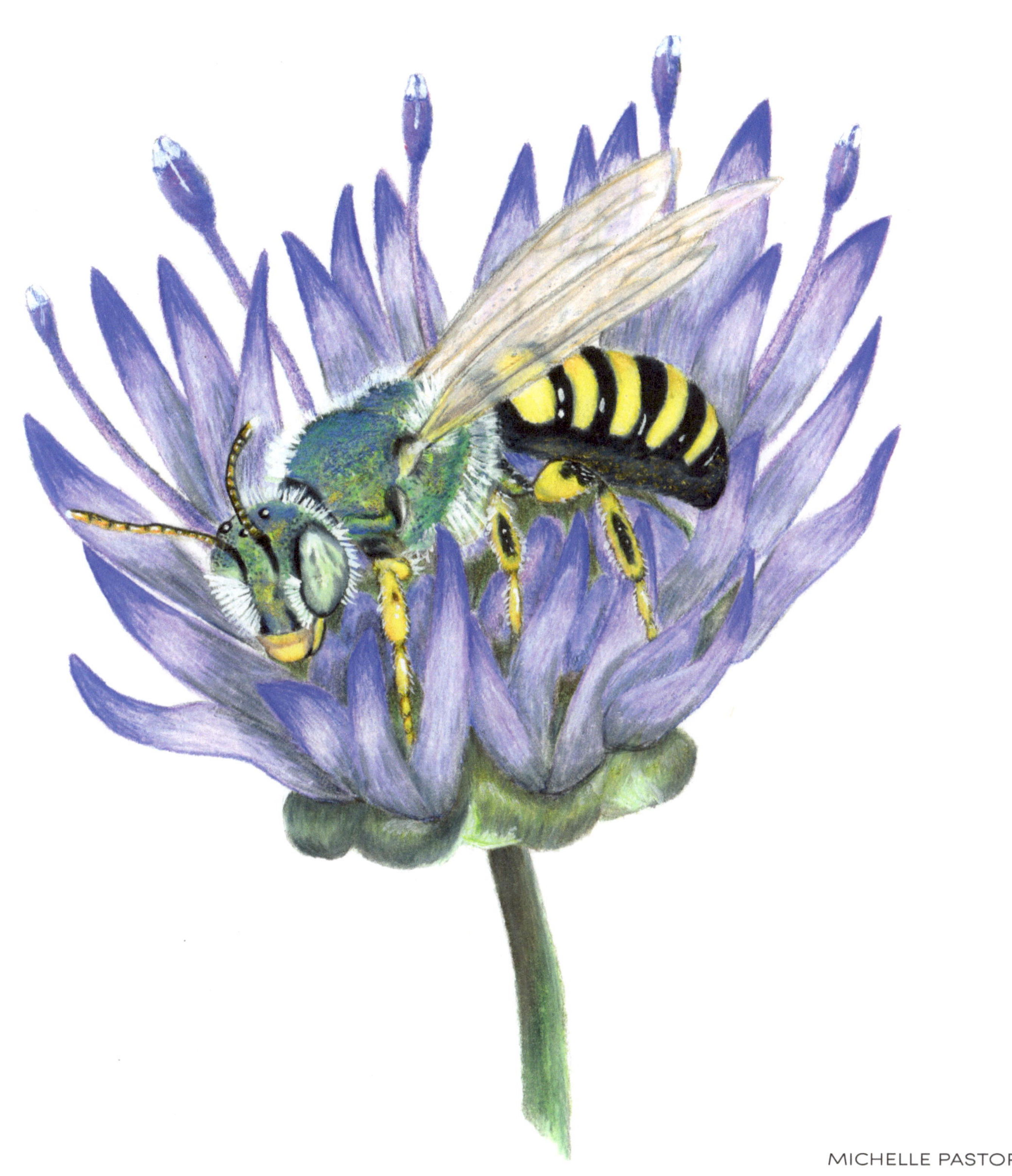

MICHELLE PASTOR

LASIOGLOSSUM sp.

&

HALICTUS tripartitus

Dancing in pollen
Searching for the correct mate
Pesticides took them

CODY AVERY

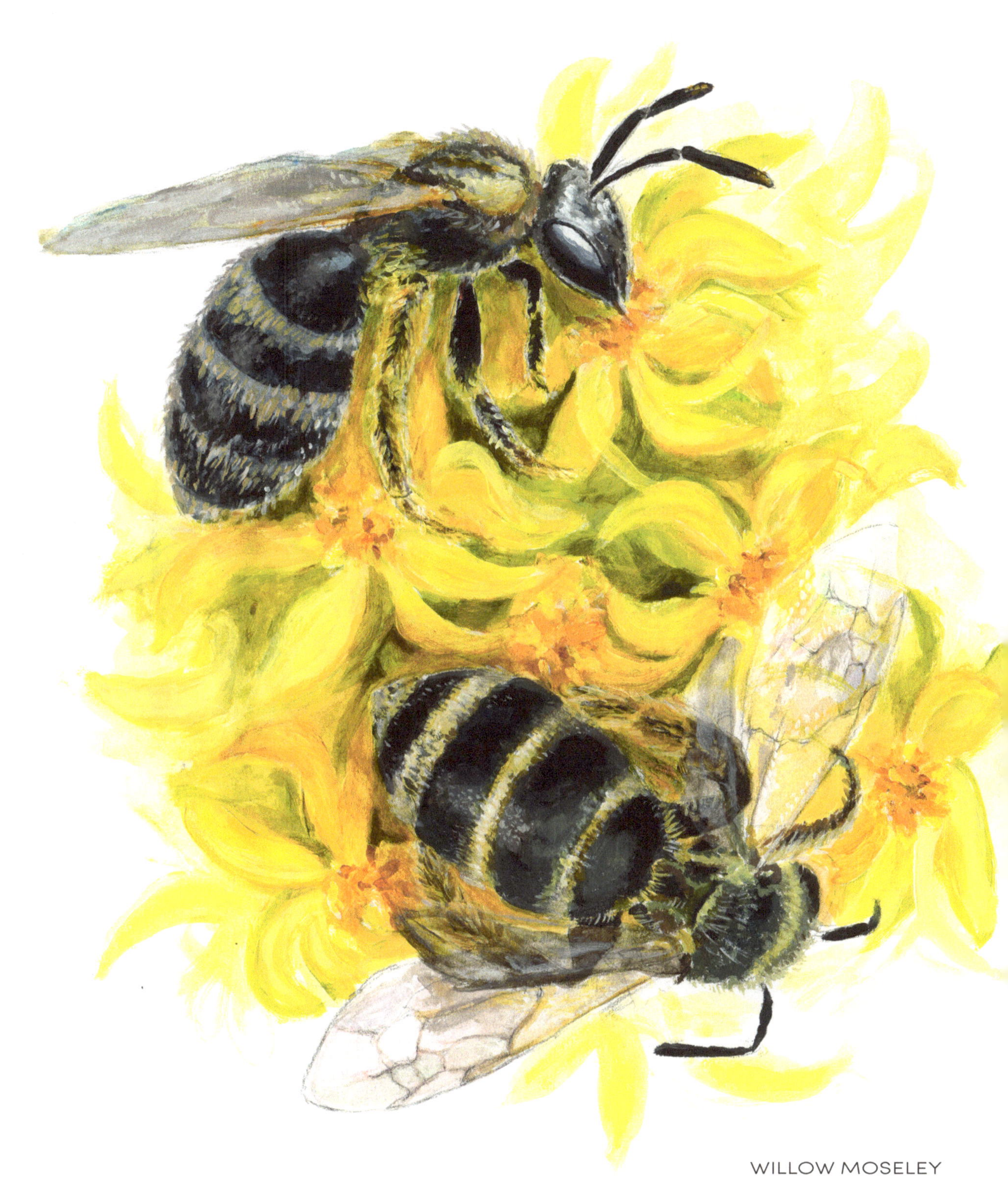

WILLOW MOSELEY

SPHECODES sp.

That shrewd cuckoo bee:
she will put her children in
where yours used to be

ANNIE STERT

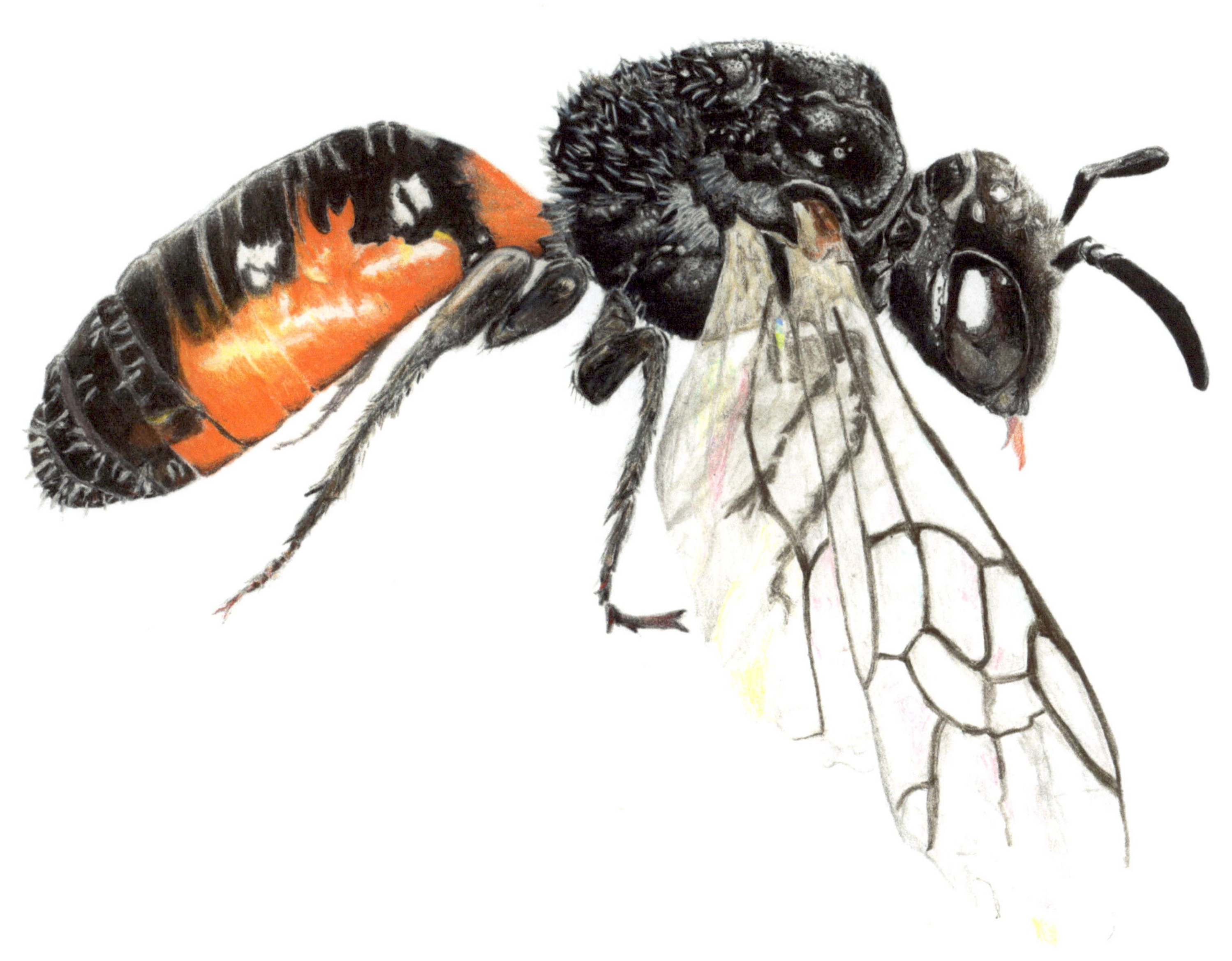

JEN SAMIS

MEGACH ILIDAE

Bees from the Megachilidae family are builders. The scientific name *Megachile* translates into *large-lipped* in Ancient Greek, referring to the strong jaws these bees possess to collect building materials. These bees are thus called the mason bees. Most species will select an above-ground cavity to build their nest. Female bees partition the nest into cells which hold a pollen provision and an egg each. The cell walls are constructed from different materials, such as masticated leaves and flowers, mud, or plant resin. The carder bees, *Anthidium*, are unique for using plant fibers. Ironically, the non-native *Anthidium manicatum* is the most well-known (it was introduced into America from Europe in the 1960s). Female carder bees scrape the hairs off wooly plants, such as lamb's ear, then bundle and carry the fibers back to the nest where the fibers will be used to fashion a cell. Carder bees exhibit curious mating behaviors. Females and males both take multiple partners, which is uncommon in the bee world. Jealous males will aggressively protect a harem of females and claim patches of flowers as terrority. They wield 5 small prongs on their abdomen, bumping against and sometimes injuring their competition! The family Megachilidae also includes some parasitic species such as *Coelioxys*, a cleptoparasite of *Megachile*. Bees within this family are also commonly domesticated for commercial pollination. For example, the Blue Orchard Bee (*Osmia lignaria*) has been adapted to pollinate almonds in the central valley of California. Several hundred orchard bees can do the work of one honey bee hive (with thousands of workers!) This family is cosmopolitan, there are hundreds of mason bee species but they stand apart from the other families because they do not carry pollen on their legs. Rather, all non-parasitic species within this group pack pollen onto the dense scopal hairs featured on the underside of their abdomen.

OSMIA
lignaria

Blue orchard bees knees
Gather pollen after freeze
Shared behind mud walls

NATALIE ANDERSON

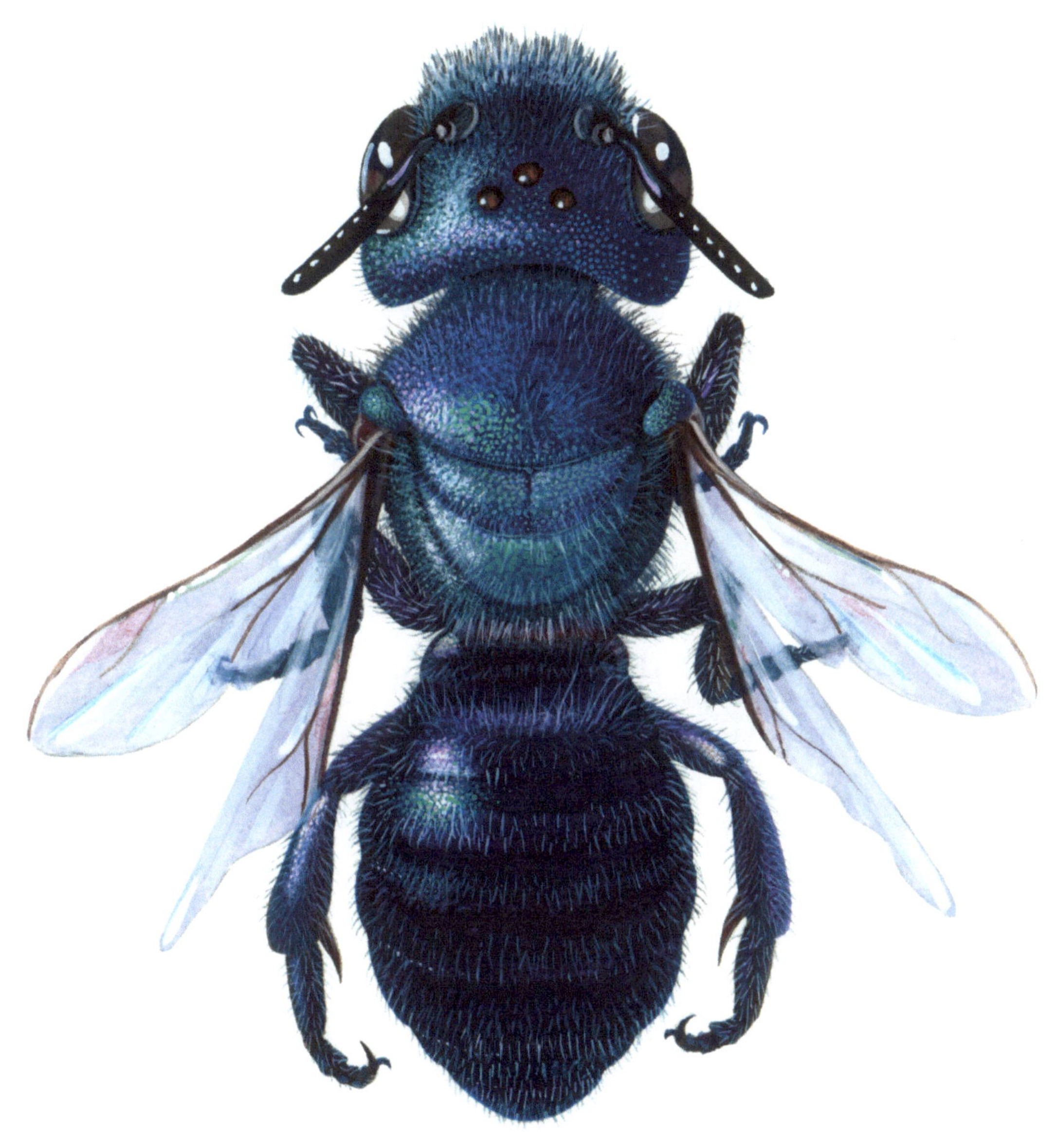

MATTIAS LANAS

OSMIA
coloradensis

Happy trails in the winter
Leg warmers year-round
Gratitude for furry bodies!

KELSEY TAYLOR

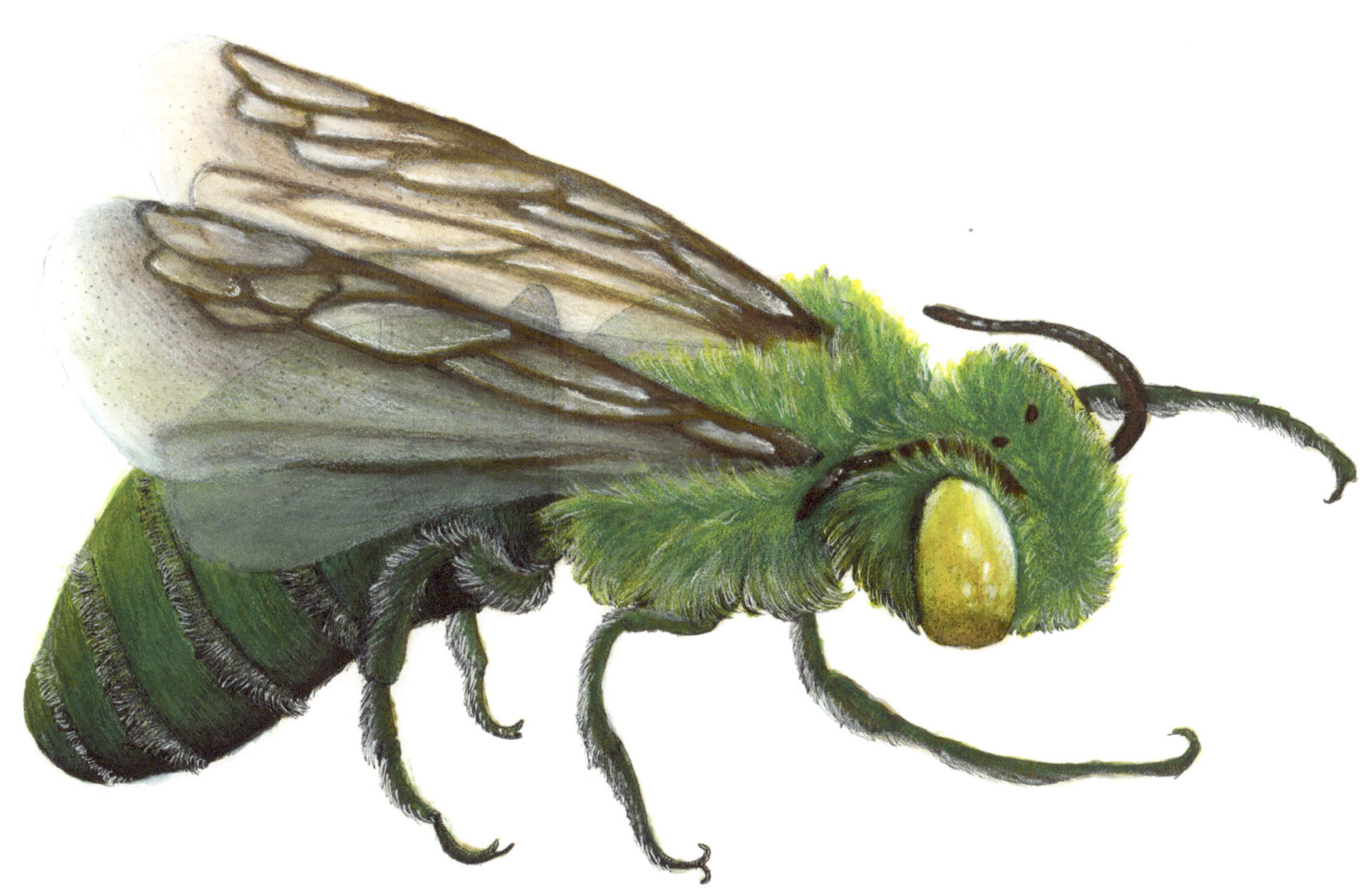

VANESSA PHAPHONE

MEGACHILE
perihirta

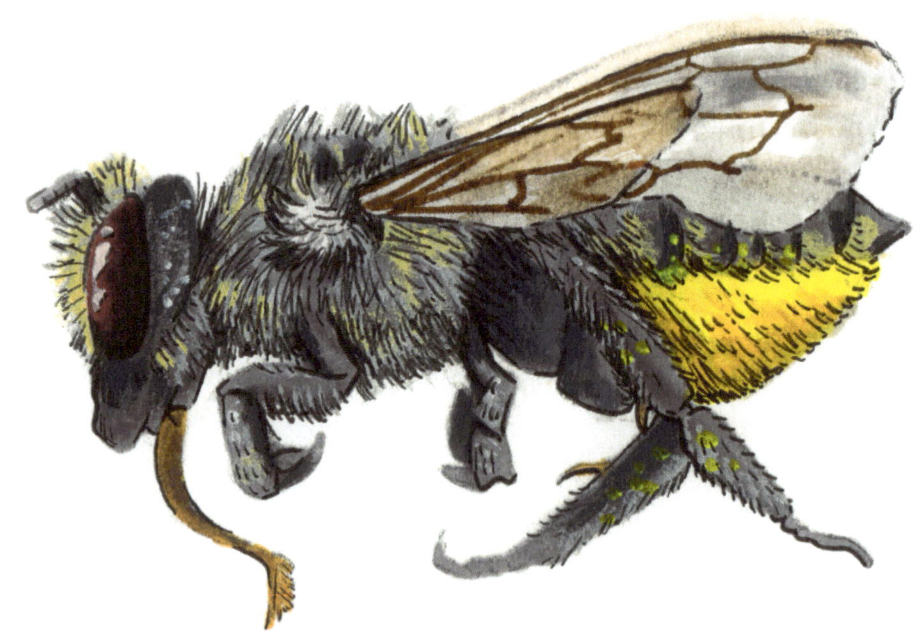

solitary bee
the seventy-five percent
unseen and unheard

ALEX PERROTTI

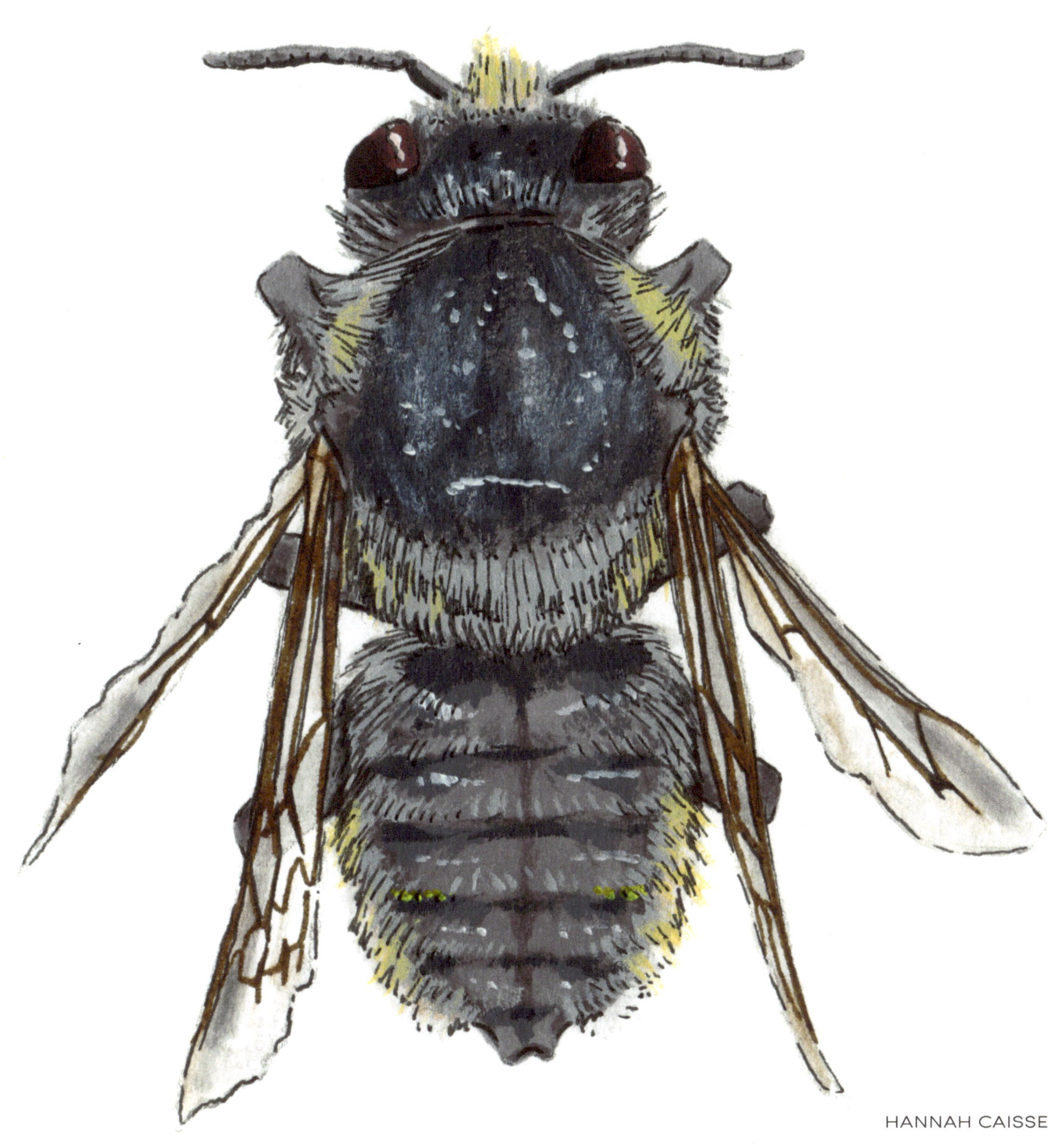

HANNAH CAISSE

ANTHIDIUM
manicatum

what magic you bring,
you dance in tiny flowers
and the world can eat

CARLY HARROWER

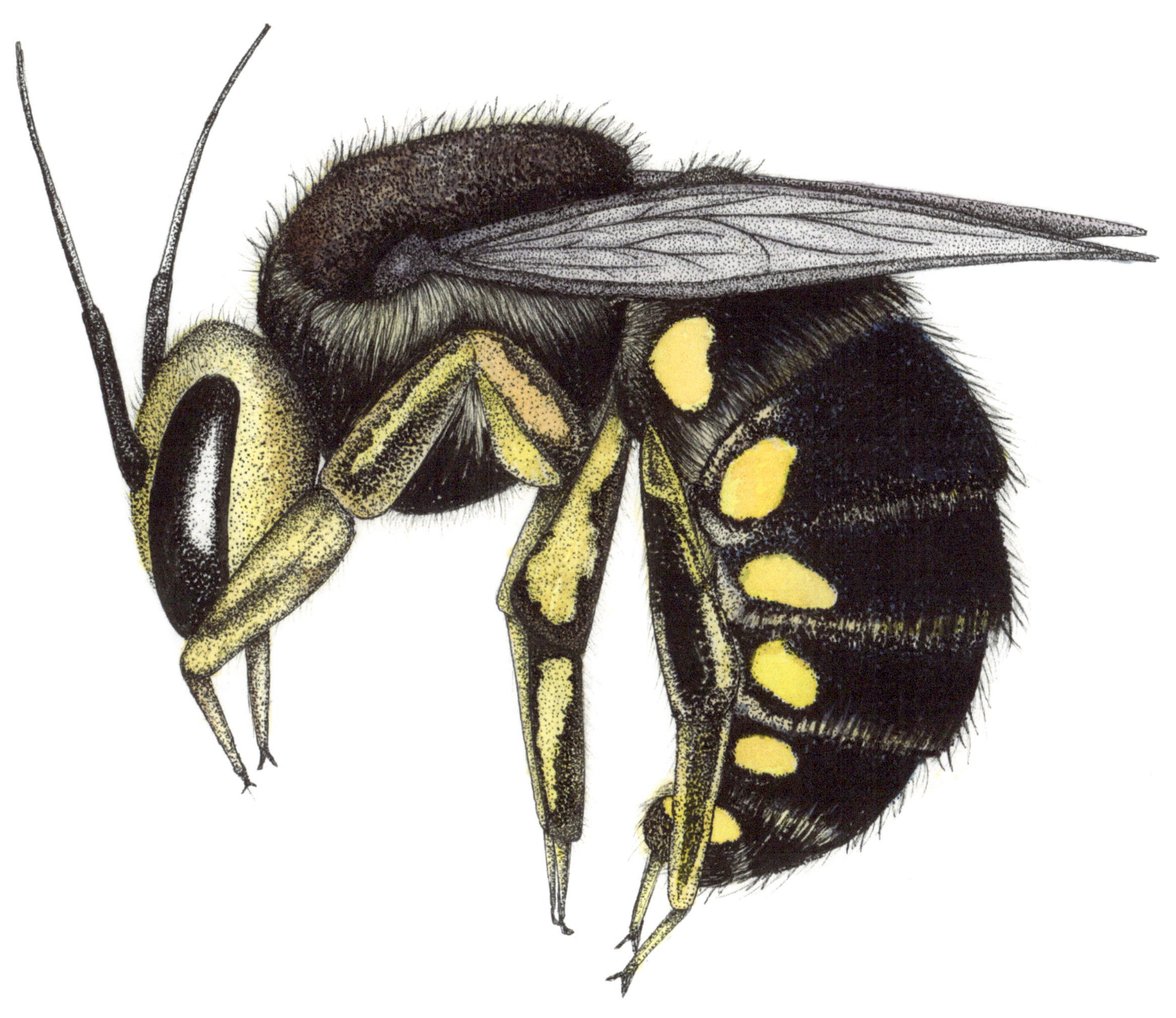

JANELLE MANLAPAS

COELIOXYS
rufitarsis

Flowers came early
We drop hungry, forgotten
Suffer with me now

JUNIPER HARROWER

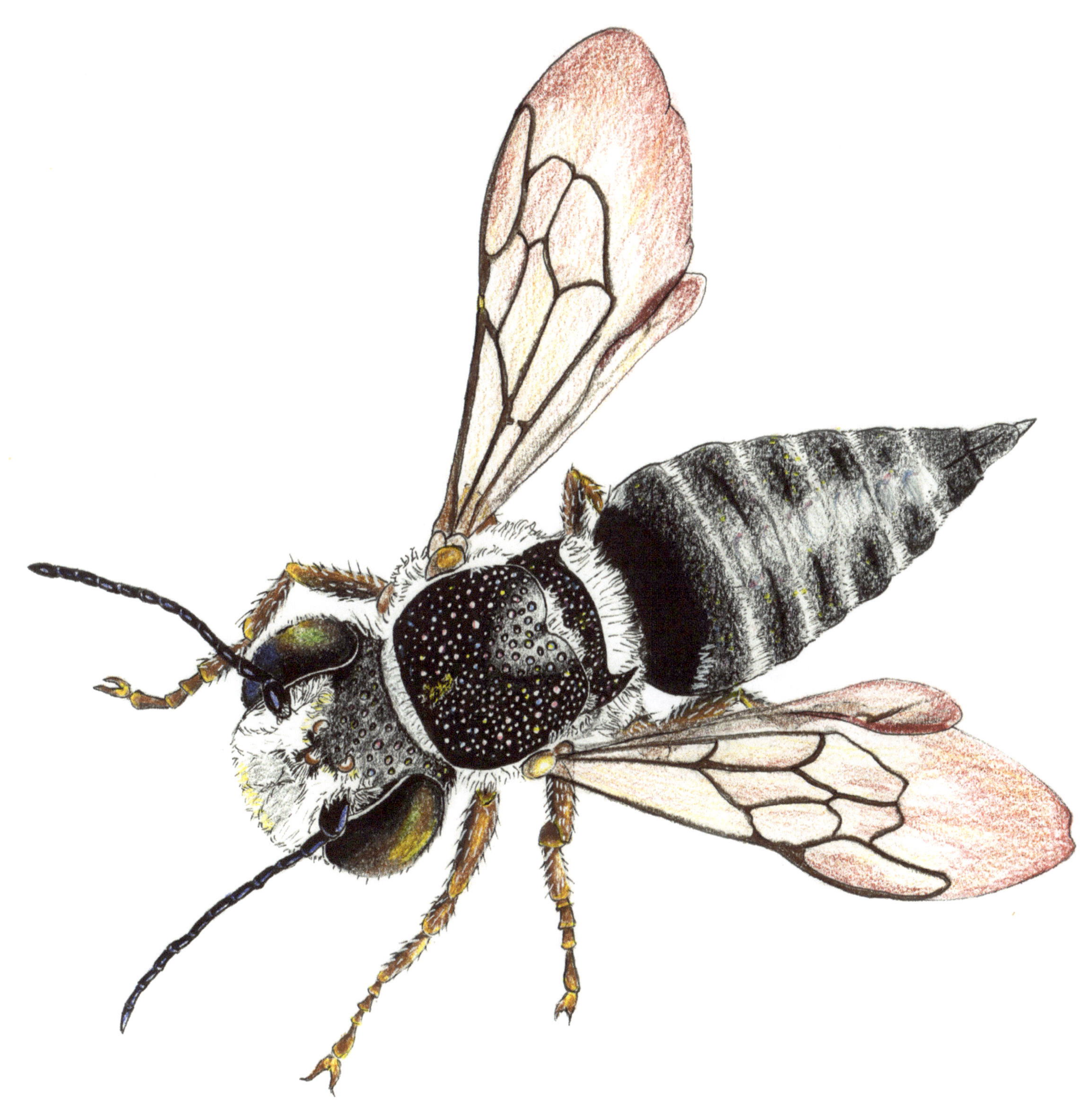
ALIYA CACANINDIN

BEE DECLINE

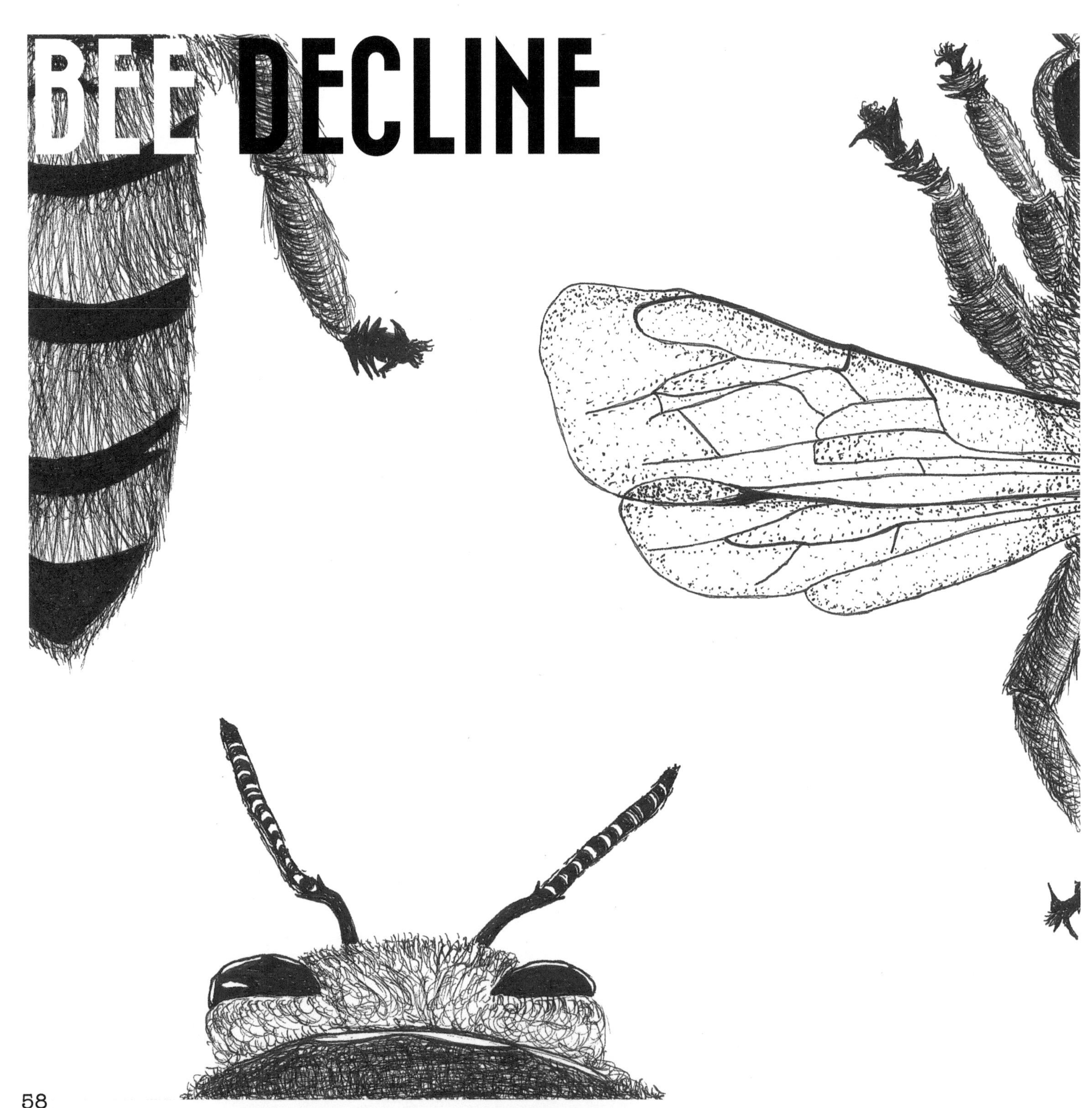

The disappearance of honey bees, known as "Colony Collapse Disorder," has been the focus of much scientific and media attention in recent years. However, bee biologists suspect that wild bees are vulnerable to the same stressors. While it is challenging to locate and study bees in the wild, scientists point to the endangered status and possible extinction of several native species, especially U.S. bumble bees. Bee decline not only threatens the delivery of pollination to native plants and agricultural crops, but is also devastating if we value bees simply for being bees. So why are bees dying? Parasites, pesticides, and a lack of flowers.

More than 20 RNA viruses have been found in honey bees and wild bees. Often, the name of a virus hints at what symptoms it causes (Deformed Wing Virus, Black Queen Cell Virus, Chronic Bee Paralysis Virus, etc.). In addition to viruses, bees might encounter bacterial and fungal diseases (Foulbrood and Chalkbrood) and both small and large parasites (from the microsporidian Nosema to blood-sucking Varroa mites). These parasites and pathogens may be symptomless or expressed by a range of symptoms, including physical abnormalities, trembling, dysentery, dead larvae, and premature mortality. Alone, these parasites and pathogens do not necessary result in death. However, bees that are weakened due to pesticide exposure, poor diets, and unsustainable beekeeping practices are more likely to succumb to disease. It is the combination of these different stressors that results in bee decline.

One of the biggest threats to wild bee populations in California is industrialized agriculture. Large-scale monoculture farms, characterized by the cultivation of a single crop type, only provide bloom for very short windows of time (temporal gluts of a single pollen and nectar type). Because monoculture farming requires intensive tilling of the soil and weed removal, bees lack the habitat they need for nesting. Because monoculture farming often results in pest problems, these farms are often heavily managed with pesticides, fungicides, and herbicides, with unintended but harmful consequences for bees. And because bees cannot naturally live in these environments, beekeepers export domesticated honey bees, bumble bees, mason bees, and leafcutter bees to farms for pollination. The introduction of these managed bees results in spillover of parasites and pathogens to wild, local bee populations. Both wild and domesticated bees in these environments are just getting hammered. While organic farming is a step in the right direction, organic certification does not preclude organically-managed monoculture farms. An organic farm is thus not necessarily a bee-friendly farm, especially because some organic pesticides, such as pyrethroids, are extremely toxic to bees.

Thankfully, change is on the horizon. Many beekeepers and farmers in California are taking steps to reduce harm to bees. They are limiting agrochemical sprays and joining "Bee Better" certification programs to protect pollinators. Change is also happening in urban cities by people just like you. Community initiatives promoting bee friendly urban gardens and city-wide bans of pesticides make a difference. But the reality is that we have to push harder. We have to rethink what we eat and how we want our food grown if want to save California's bees.

BLOSSOMS FOR BEES

Bees eat pollen and nectar. While some bees specialize on specific groups of flowers (*oligolectic*), others forage widely (*polylectic*). Some bees will travel extremely far to forage (honey bees can travel several miles!), while others are limited to foraging locally near their nest. To provide bees with the protein (pollen) and carbohydrates (nectar) they need to stay healthy, plant a diversity of flowers. Group patches of the same plant species together instead of spacing them out, this will be more attractive to bees. To ensure something in bloom year-round, plant both early-flowering and late-flowering ornamentals. Don't forget to dead-head your flowers to promote a longer bloom. You can't go wrong if you populate your garden with mints and salvias (*Lamiaceae*), daisies and sunflowers (*Asteraceae*), roses and fruit trees (*Rosaceae*), buckwheats (*Polygonaceae*), verbenas (*Verbenaceae*) and borages (*Boraginaceae*). For detailed recommendations, check out the "Resources" page at the back of this book.

PLANTS AND THEIR POLLINATORS

Pink Cosmos	🟡	Melissodes, Megachilid, Halictid, Honey Bee
California poppies	🟤	Halictid, Bumble Bee, Honey Bee
Scabiosa & Bachelor Button	🔵	Halictid, Melissodes, Honey Bee,
Squash	🟢	Peponapis, Honey Bee
Borage	🟠	Bumble Bee, Honey Bee
Sunflower	🟣	Melissodes, Halictid, Megachilid, Bumble Bee, Honey Bee
Apple Tree	🔵	Halictid, Osmia, Bumble Bee, Honey Bee

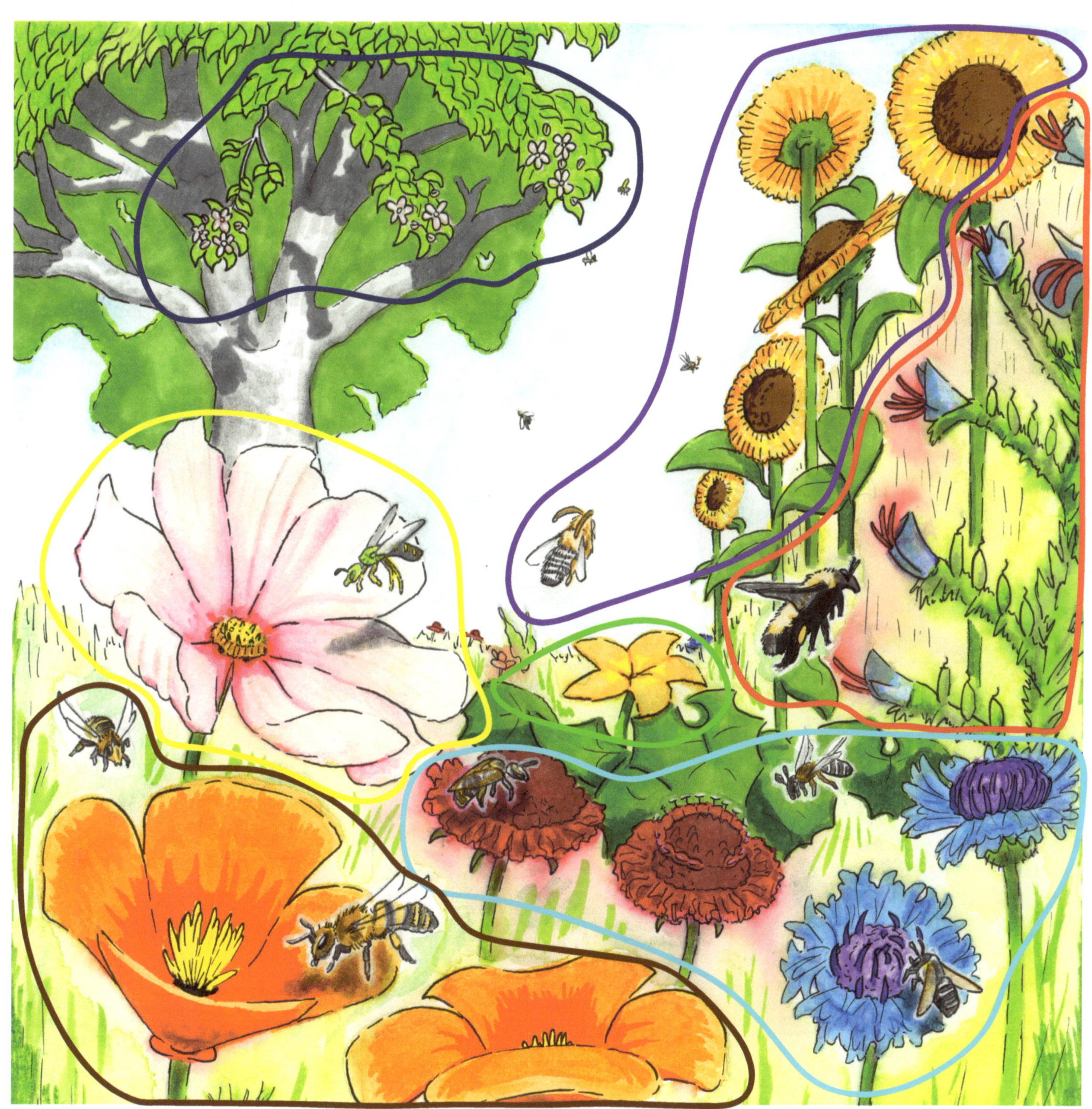

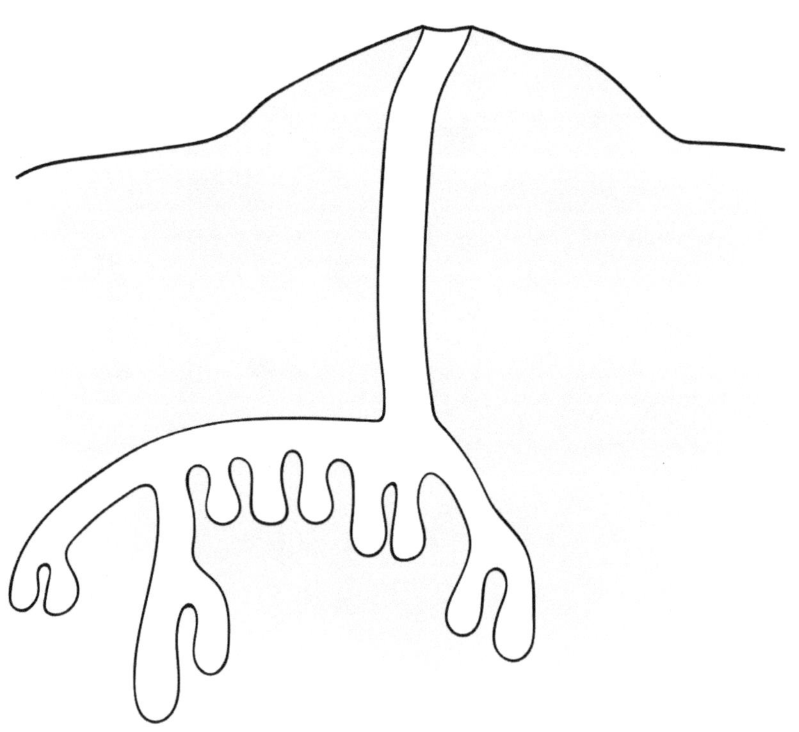

A BEE'S BUNKHOUSE

Bees construct nests as a place to rear their young. They will select a pre-existing cavity or make it themselves, either above-ground or below-ground. Depending on the species, bees will either work together or alone to construct nests. Social bees such as honey bees and bumble bees have worker bees that are in charge of making the nest, while solitary bee species such as the mason bees are on their own. Regardless, there are some similarities in nest construction. Nests are comprised of brood cells that a mother bees will provision with pollen and nectar before laying an egg. Some bees are progressive feeders and feed larvae at repeated intervals, (like honey bees and bumble bees) while others are mass provisioners - they put in one pollen provision for each egg and are done all at once (like most sweat bees). Sometimes these food provisions are liquidy, resembling a soup of pollen and nectar. Other times they are a firm, round mass. To protect their offspring and the provisions they collect, female bees will collect and line their cells with different materials such as propolis, leaves, petals, and even mud.

Bees will avoid nesting (and even abandon their nest) if heavily disturbed. To make your farm or garden habitable for bees that nest below-ground, make sure to leave a few areas with patchy or bare soil. Tilling, heavy mulching, or walking over these areas will deter bees. Because above-ground bees utilize pithy stems, reeds, and cavities, you can actually provide these materials for them by adding an "insect hotel" to your garden. You can construct these shelters in all shapes and sizes using old clay and stone bricks, tiles, bamboo reed, bark, logs with long holes drilled in. Place your insect hotel where it will be protected from the elements but still get plenty of sun. Because insects aggregate at hotels, make sure to occasionally clean it and swap out the materials to prevent the spread of disease. If you experiment with different materials you may also find beneficial lacewings, ladybugs, and butterflies taking advantage of your insect hotel!

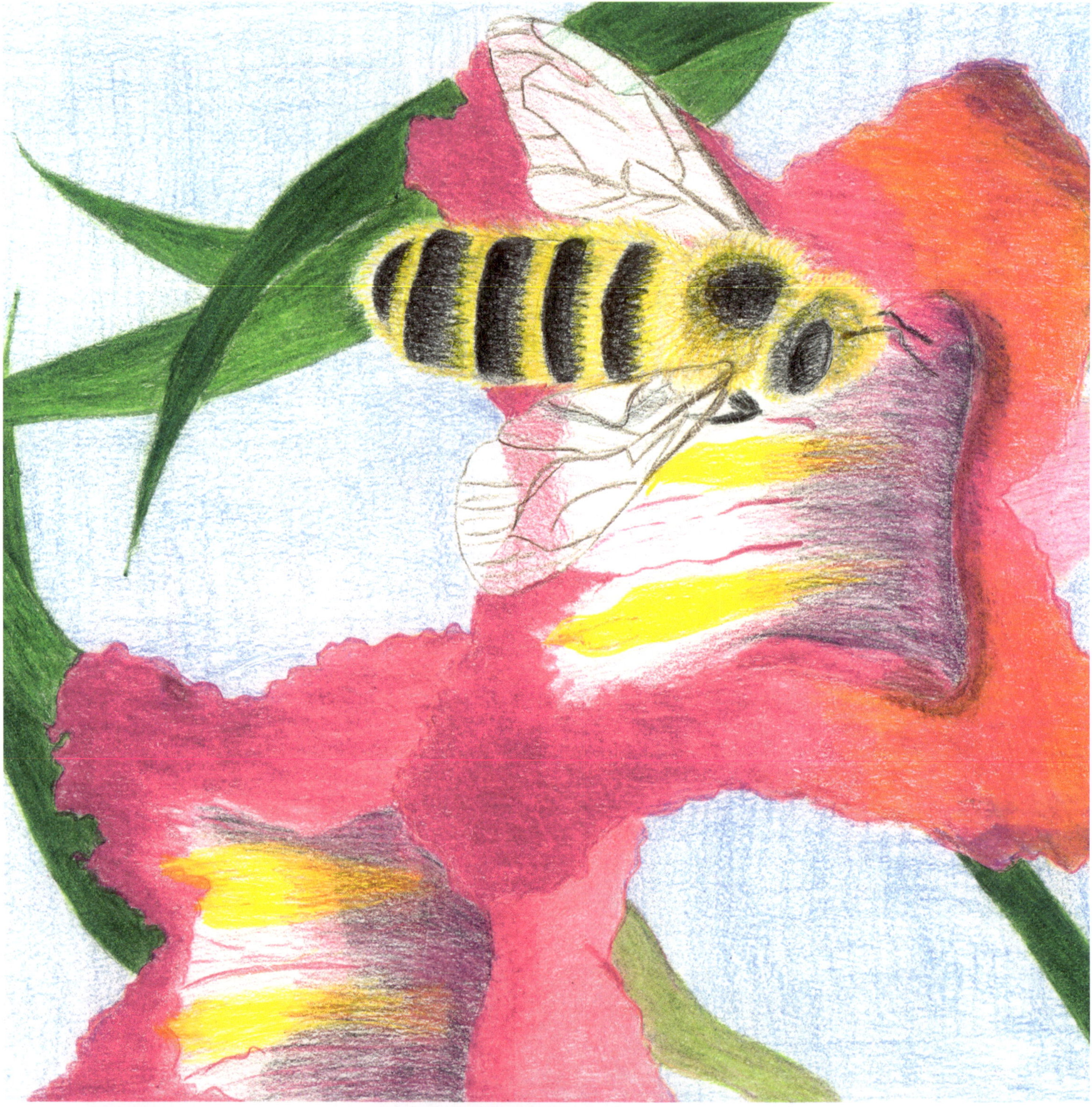

RESOURCES

We referenced the following literature to write the content for this book. These texts also serve as great resources if you would like to learn more about bees.

Bees of the World by Charles D. Michener
A comprehensive and excellent source of information about bee biology, ecology, and classification. Includes information about bee nesting, evolution, social behavior, and more. Perfect for any bee lover, this book includes references for those wanting to dig even further.

The Bee Genera of North and Central America by Charles D. Michener, Ronald J. McGinley, and Bryan N. Danforth
Includes identification keys to bees at the genus level. Written by top-notch experts and absolutely necessary for biologists and serious academic-level bee identification effort.

California Bees & Blooms: A guide for gardeners and naturalists by Gordon W. Frankie, Robbin W. Thorp, Rollin E. Coville, and Barbara Ertter
Describes the distinct behaviors, preferred flowers, and enemies of 22 common bee genera in California. The book includes 53 bee-friendly plants and how to grow them.

www.helpabee.org by Gordon Frankie's research group at the University of California, Berkeley
A complete guide for gardeners, horticulturalists, and farmers growing their own bee-friendly gardens and plots! Includes detailed lists of bees and the plants that they prefer. Our go-to for selecting blossoms for bees.

www.greatsunflower.org by Gretchen LeBuhn's research group at San Francisco State University
You can help scientists study pollination by joining this citizen science project! After signing up, you plant flowers and then send in data about the bees you observe directly via the website. This project helps scientists study urban bee populations. The website also includes useful information about pesticides, evaluating pollinator habitat, and how you can help declining bee populations.

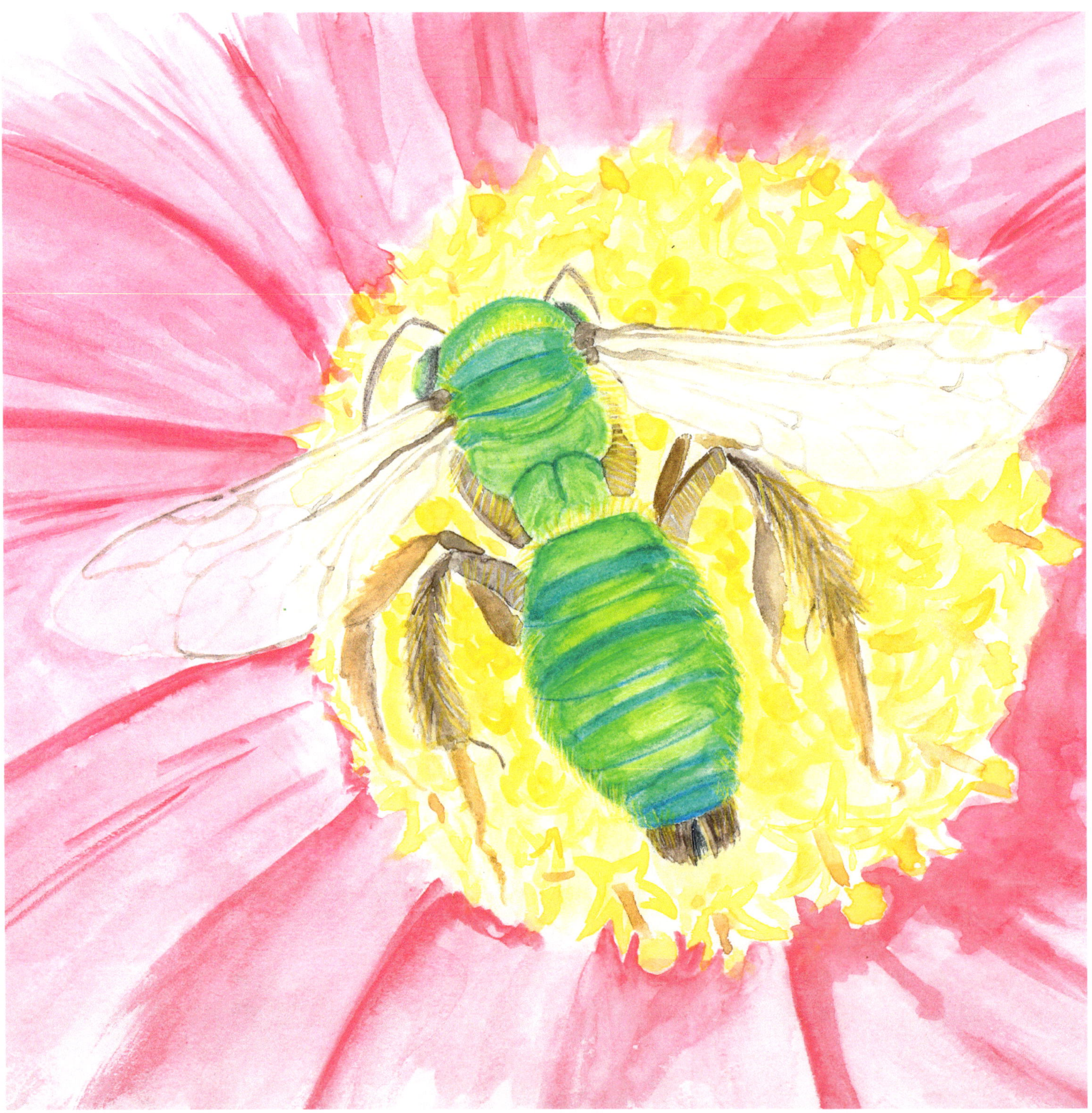

www.ingramcontent.com/pod-product-compliance
Lightning Source LLC
Chambersburg PA
CBHW042150030726
47599CB00004B/688